READING EXPLORER

TEACHER'S GUIDE

NANCY DOUGLAS • DAVID BOHLKE • KRISTIN SHERMAN
HELEN HUNTLEY • BRUCE ROGERS • PAUL MACINTYRE

Second Edition

NATIONAL GEOGRAPHIC LEARNING | CENGAGE Learning

Australia • Brazil • Japan • Korea • Mexico • Singapore • Spain • United Kingdom • United States

Reading Explorer Teacher's Guide 5
Second Edition

Nancy Douglas, David Bohlke, Kristin Sherman, Helen Huntley, Bruce Rogers, and Paul MacIntyre

Publisher: Andrew Robinson

Executive Editor: Sean Bermingham

Senior Development Editor: Derek Mackrell

Development Editor: Christopher Street

Editorial Assistant: Dylan Mitchell

Director of Global Marketing: Ian Martin

Product Marketing Manager: Anders Bylund

Senior Director of Production: Michael Burggren

Senior Content Project Manager: Tan Jin Hock

Manufacturing Planner: Mary Beth Hennebury

Compositor: SPi Global

Cover Design: Creative Director: Christopher Roy, Art Director: Scott Baker, Senior Designer: Michael Rosenquest

Photo Credits: Cover, 1 Sasha Gusov/Axiom Photographic Agency/Getty Images, **3** Thomas Dressler/age fotostock

ISBN-13: 978-1-285-84705-4

National Geographic Learning
20 Channel Center Street
Boston, MA 02210
USA

Cengage Learning is a leading provider of customized learning solutions with office locations around the globe, including Singapore, the United Kingdom, Australia, Mexico, Brazil, and Japan. Locate your local office at: **international.cengage.com/region**

Cengage Learning products are represented in Canada by Nelson Education, Ltd.

Visit National Geographic Learning online at **NGL.Cengage.com**

Visit our corporate website at **www.cengage.com**

Printed in the United States of America
Print Number: 02 Print Year: 2017

Contents

Take a tour of

Reading Explorer

Thank you for choosing to use Reading Explorer Book 5. Here are 10 steps to help you get familiar with the course:

1. First, look at the list of **Contents** on page 3 of the Student Book. You'll see the book is organized into 12 units. The book can be used for a short course of 24–36 hours using just the core units or can be extended for longer courses, for example, by using the **Viewing** activities in class.

Contents

2. Look at the **Scope and Sequence** on pages 4–5 of the Student Book. You'll see that each unit is based on a theme of general interest, for example, "Human Body." Within each unit are two lessons, each based around a reading passage. You'll also note the range of reading skills and vocabulary building sections covered in the book.

Scope and Sequence

Unit	Theme	Reading	Reading Skill	Vocabulary Building	Video
1	Collapse	A: Secrets of the Maya B: The Collapse of Angkor	A: Understanding Infographics B: Evaluating the Strengths of Arguments	A: Word Partnership: *sacrifice* B: Word Link: *reg-*	Temples in the Jungle
2	Beyond Earth	A: Cosmic Dawn B: Planet Hunters: Are We Alone?	A: Determining the Main Idea of Paragraphs B: Understanding Cause and Effect Relationships	A: Word Link: *mit* B: Word Link: *com-*	Comet Watchers
3	Health and Genes	A: Mending Broken Hearts B: The War on Allergies	A: Scanning for Details (I) B: Using Concept Maps	A: Usage: *exacerbate and compound* B: Thesaurus: *tolerate*	Fighting Malaria
4	Vanishing Cities	A: City Under Siege B: Rising Seas	A: Recognizing Literal vs. Figurative Language B: Reading a Text Critically	A: Usage: *complement and compliment* B: Word Link: *poli*	Time and Tide
5	Eco-Living	A: Carbon Footprint B: Plugging into the Sun	A: Distinguishing Main Ideas and Supporting Information B: Identifying Similarities and Differences	A: Word Partnership: *obstacle* B: Word Partnership: *premium*	Eco-Detectives
6	Wildlife in Trouble	A: Quicksilver B: Building the Ark	A: Identifying Homonyms B: Understanding Root Words of Greek and Latin Origin	A: Word Link: *turb* B: Thesaurus: *imminent*	Life on Ice
7	Human Body	A: Secrets of the Brain B: Human Bionics	A: Understanding the Use of the Passive Voice B: Distinguishing Fact from Opinion	A: Word Partnership: *unprecedented* B: Word Link: *val*	Bionic Mountaineer
8	Social Behavior	A: The Genius of Swarms B: Of Ants and Humans	A: Understanding Inference B: Scanning for Details (II)	A: Usage: *code and protocol* B: Word Partnership: *fatal*	Monarch Migration
9	Creativity	A: Decoding Leonardo B: The Power of Writing	A: Relating Textual Information to a Map B: Understanding Chronological Sequence	A: Word Partnership: *deny* B: Word Link: *man/manu*	The Birthplace of Writing
10	Elements and Toxins	A: Hidden Hazards B: Element Hunters	A: Identifying Theory and Fact B: Understanding Long Sentences	A: Usage: *albeit* B: Word Link: *counter-*	Secrets of Toothpaste
11	Islam and the West	A: The World of Süleyman the Magnificent B: When the Moors Ruled Spain	A: Creating a Mental Map of a Text B: Inferring an Author's Attitude	A: Word Link: *bi-* B: Word Partnership: *violate*	Heritage of Spain
12	Wealth and Finance	A: From Clams to Credit Cards B: Gold Fever	A: Applying Information from a Text B: Identifying Coherence Devices	A: Word Partnership: *obligation* B: Word Link: *-ship*	The Art Smuggler

Scope and Sequence 5

3. Read **Welcome to Reading Explorer!** on page 6 of the Student Book. It highlights the new features of the Second Edition and how they help students to become active, fluent readers.

Welcome to Reading Explorer!

In this book, you'll travel the globe, explore different cultures, and discover new ways of looking at the world. You'll also become a better reader!

What's new in the Second Edition?

New and updated topics
Explore the ruins of ancient civilizations, the effects of rising seas, and join the race to discover new elements.

New Reading Skills section
Learn how to read strategically—and think critically as you read.

Expanded Viewing section
Apply your language skills when you watch a specially adapted National Geographic video.

Now you're ready to explore your world!

6 Introduction

4. Skim through a **Unit** of the Student Book and compare it against the Unit Walkthrough on the following pages of this Teacher's Guide. Each unit is accompanied in the Teacher's Guide by teaching suggestions and background notes (see pages 20–79).

5. Turn to one of the **Reading Passages** in the Student Book (e.g., Student Book page 9). The reading passages are all adapted from authentic National Geographic sources, which are listed in the **Credits** on page 272 of the Student Book. Each reading passage is also available as an audio recording in the **Classroom Audio CD/DVD Package** as well as in the **Online Workbook**, providing a useful model for pronunciation and intonation.

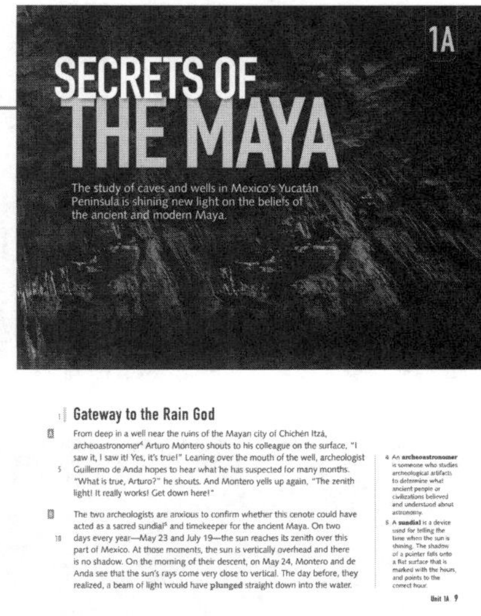

6. You'll note in each reading passage that useful, high-frequency words are highlighted in red. A complete list of these **Target Vocabulary** words is available online at NGL.Cengage.com/readingexplorer. For suggestions on teaching vocabulary, see pages 14–16 of this Teacher's Guide.

7. Check out the **Video clips** on the **Classroom Audio CD/DVD Package**. The clips can be used with the **Viewing** section at the end of each Student Book unit, and also with the video comprehension activities in the **Online Workbook**. The scripts for the videos are available at NGL.Cengage.com/readingexplorer. You'll see that the video narration recycles many of the target vocabulary items. For ideas on using video in class, see pages 16–17 of this Teacher's Guide.

8. Check out the range of ancillary components of the course. The **Online Workbook** contains the 12 video clips, and a variety of interactive comprehension and vocabulary activities. The activities are self-grading and provide reinforcement for the language presented in each unit. Additional learning and teaching resources are available online at NGL.Cengage.com/readingexplorer.

9. An **Assessment CD-ROM** containing ExamView® question banks is available for teachers who want to create customized tests or give students additional language practice. See page 17 of this Teacher's Guide for suggestions on assessing learners' progress.

10. Finally, note that each of the Student Books and Teacher's Guides are also available as eBooks. For more information, go to NGL.Cengage.com/readingexplorer.

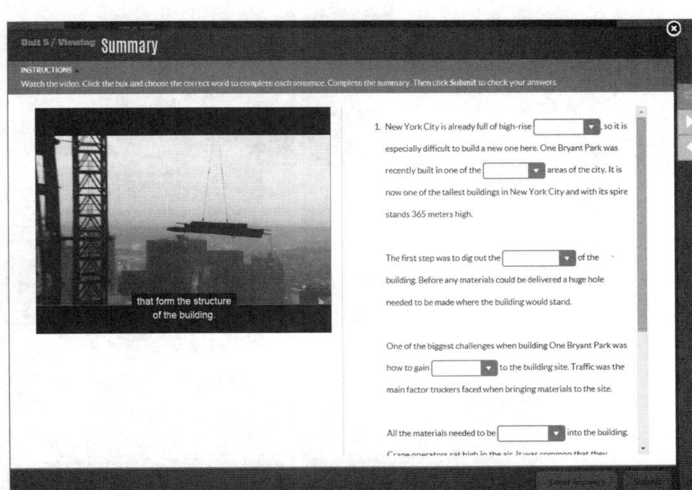

Unit Walkthrough

Warm Up discussion questions help to raise learners' interest in the unit theme and activate learners' prior knowledge.

Before You Read tasks introduce key terms and content that learners will encounter in the reading passage, and develop previewing skills such as skimming and making predictions.

Maps, captions, charts, and graphs develop learners' visual literacy—their ability to decode graphic information effectively.

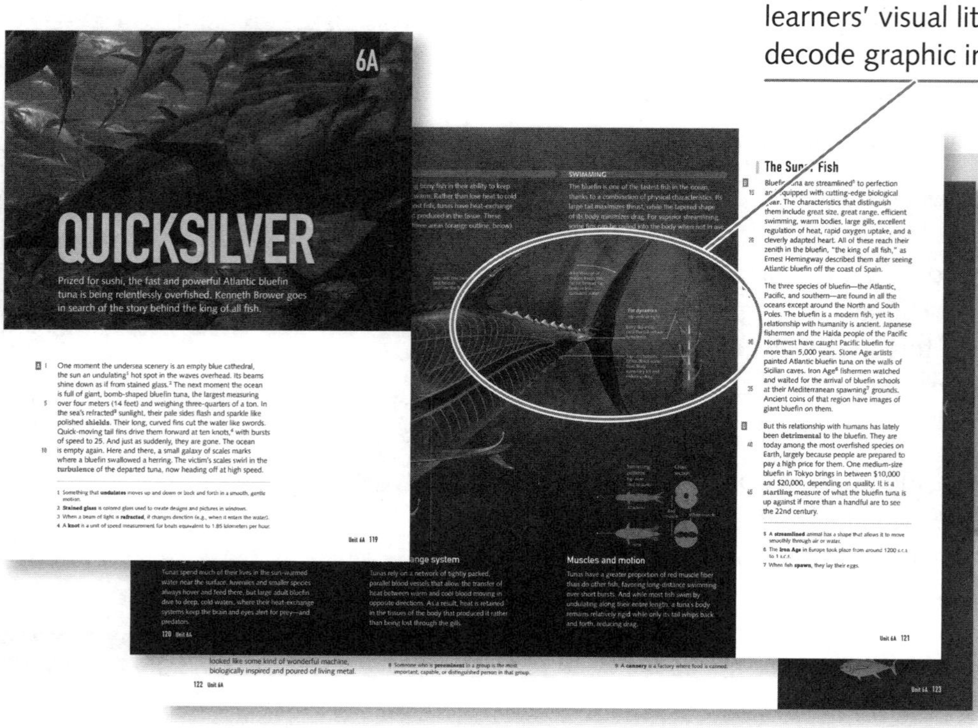

Each **Reading Passage** is adapted from an authentic National Geographic source; the language has been carefully graded and the reading contains ten high-frequency "target vocabulary" items.

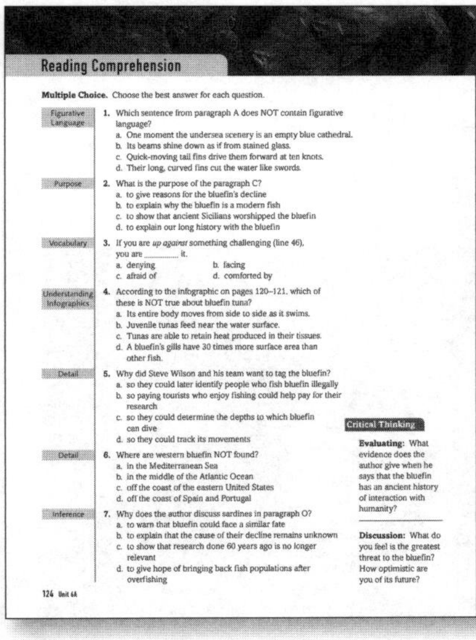
Reading Comprehension

Multiple Choice. Choose the best answer for each question.

Figurative Language
1. Which sentence from paragraph A does NOT contain figurative language?
   a. One moment the undersea scenery is an empty blue cathedral.
   b. Its beams shine down as if from stained glass.
   c. Quick-moving tail fins drive them forward at ten knots.
   d. Their long, curved fins cut the water like swords.

Purpose
2. What is the purpose of the paragraph C?
   a. to give reasons for the bluefin's decline
   b. to explain why the bluefin is a modern fish
   c. to show that ancient Sicilians worshipped the bluefin
   d. to explain our long history with the bluefin

Vocabulary
3. If you are *up against* something challenging (line 46), you are ________ it.
   a. denying b. facing
   c. afraid of d. comforted by

Understanding Infographics
4. According to the infographic on pages 120–121, which of these is NOT true about bluefin tuna?
   a. Its entire body moves from side to side as it swims.
   b. Juvenile tunas feed near the water surface.
   c. Tunas are able to retain heat produced in their tissues.
   d. A bluefin's gills have 30 times more surface area than other fish.

Detail
5. Why did Steve Wilson and his team want to tag the bluefin?
   a. so they could later identify people who fish bluefin illegally
   b. so paying tourists who enjoy fishing could help pay for their research
   c. so they could determine the depths to which bluefin can dive
   d. so they could track its movements

Detail
6. Where are western bluefin NOT found?
   a. in the Mediterranean Sea
   b. in the middle of the Atlantic Ocean
   c. off the coast of the eastern United States
   d. off the coast of Spain and Portugal

Inference
7. Why does the author discuss sardines in paragraph O?
   a. to warn that bluefin could face a similar fate
   b. to explain that the cause of their decline remains unknown
   c. to show that research done 60 years ago is no longer relevant
   d. to give hope of bringing back fish populations after overfishing

Critical Thinking

Evaluating: What evidence does the author give when he says that the bluefin has an ancient history of interaction with humanity?

Discussion: What do you feel is the greatest threat to the bluefin? How optimistic are you of its future?

124 Unit 6A

Reading Comprehension activities include question types commonly found in high-stakes international exams, such as TOEFL® and TOEIC®.

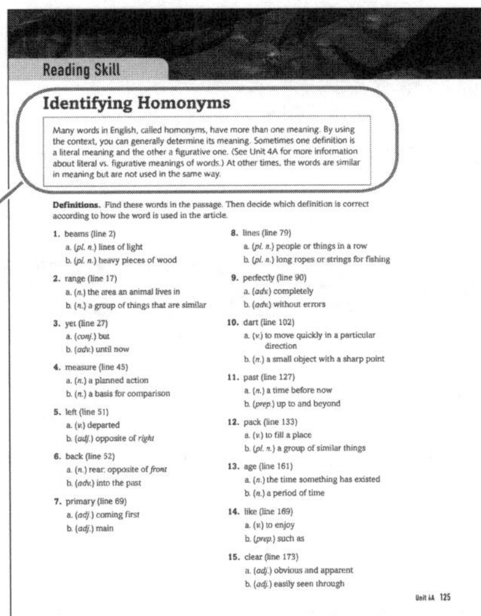
Reading Skill

Identifying Homonyms

Many words in English, called homonyms, have more than one meaning. By using the context, you can generally determine its meaning. Sometimes one definition is a literal meaning and the other a figurative one. (See Unit 4A for more information about literal vs. figurative meanings of words.) At other times, the words are similar in meaning but are not used in the same way.

Definitions. Find these words in the passage. Then decide which definition is correct according to how the word is used in the article.

1. beams (line 2)
   a. (*pl. n.*) lines of light
   b. (*pl. n.*) heavy pieces of wood
2. range (line 17)
   a. (*n.*) the area an animal lives in
   b. (*n.*) a group of things that are similar
3. yet (line 27)
   a. (*conj.*) but
   b. (*adv.*) until now
4. measure (line 45)
   a. (*n.*) a planned action
   b. (*n.*) a basis for comparison
5. left (line 51)
   a. (*v.*) departed
   b. (*adj.*) opposite of *right*
6. back (line 52)
   a. (*n.*) rear: opposite of *front*
   b. (*adv.*) into the past
7. primary (line 69)
   a. (*adj.*) coming first
   b. (*adj.*) main
8. lines (line 79)
   a. (*pl. n.*) people or things in a row
   b. (*pl. n.*) long ropes or strings for fishing
9. perfectly (line 90)
   a. (*adv.*) completely
   b. (*adv.*) without errors
10. dart (line 102)
   a. (*v.*) to move quickly in a particular direction
   b. (*n.*) a small object with a sharp point
11. past (line 127)
   a. (*n.*) a time before now
   b. (*prep.*) up to and beyond
12. pack (line 133)
   a. (*v.*) to fill a place
   b. (*pl. n.*) a group of similar things
13. age (line 161)
   a. (*n.*) the time something has existed
   b. (*n.*) a period of time
14. like (line 169)
   a. (*v.*) to enjoy
   b. (*prep.*) such as
15. clear (line 173)
   a. (*adj.*) obvious and apparent
   b. (*adj.*) easily seen through

Unit 6A 125

The text box explaining the skill often identifies signal words that make students more aware of how the text has been constructed.

Reading Skill tasks include a variety of graphic organizers, which help learners to understand the relationship between key ideas in the passage.

Each chapter presents a different Reading Skill. Examples of the skill are often drawn from the chapter's reading passage. The Reading Skill section is addressed in each chapter of the Teacher's Guide with suggestions for further development.

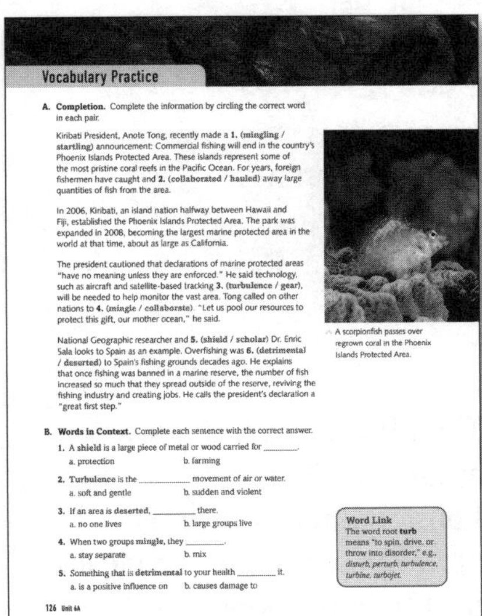
Vocabulary Practice

A. Completion. Complete the information by circling the correct word in each pair.

Kiribati President, Anote Tong, recently made a **1. (mingling / startling)** announcement: Commercial fishing will end in the country's Phoenix Islands Protected Area. These islands represent some of the most pristine coral reefs in the Pacific Ocean. For years, foreign fishermen have caught and **2. (collaborated / hauled)** away large quantities of fish from the area.

In 2006, Kiribati, an island nation halfway between Hawaii and Fiji, established the Phoenix Islands Protected Area. The park was expanded in 2008, becoming the largest marine protected area in the world at that time, about as large as California.

The president cautioned that declarations of marine protected areas "have no meaning unless they are enforced." He said technology, such as aircraft and satellite-based tracking **3. (turbulence / gear)**, will be needed to help monitor the vast area. Tong called on other nations to **4. (mingle / collaborate)**. "Let us pool our resources to protect this gift, our mother ocean," he said.

National Geographic researcher and **5. (shield / scholar)** Dr. Enric Sala looks to Spain as an example. Overfishing was **6. (detrimental / deserted)** to Spain's fishing grounds decades ago. He explains that once fishing was banned in a marine reserve, the number of fish increased so much that they spread outside of the reserve, reviving the fishing industry and creating jobs. He calls the president's declaration a "great first step."

A scorpionfish passes over regrown coral in the Phoenix Islands Protected Area.

B. Words in Context. Complete each sentence with the correct answer.

1. A **shield** is a large piece of metal or wood carried for ________.
   a. protection b. farming
2. **Turbulence** is the ________ movement of air or water.
   a. soft and gentle b. sudden and violent
3. If an area is **deserted**, ________ there.
   a. no one lives b. large groups live
4. When two groups **mingle**, they ________.
   a. stay separate b. mix
5. Something that is **detrimental** to your health ________ it.
   a. is a positive influence on b. causes damage to

Word Link
The word root **turb** means "to spin, drive, or throw into disorder," e.g., *disturb, perturb, turbulence, turbine, turbojet.*

126 Unit 6A

The **Vocabulary Practice** page in each chapter focuses on the ten target vocabulary items, giving students the chance to encounter them in different contexts and understand their meanings.

Unit Walkthrough (Continued)

Background information on the subject of the passage gives students a better perspective.

A second reading in each unit expands learners' knowledge of the unit theme and further builds vocabulary.

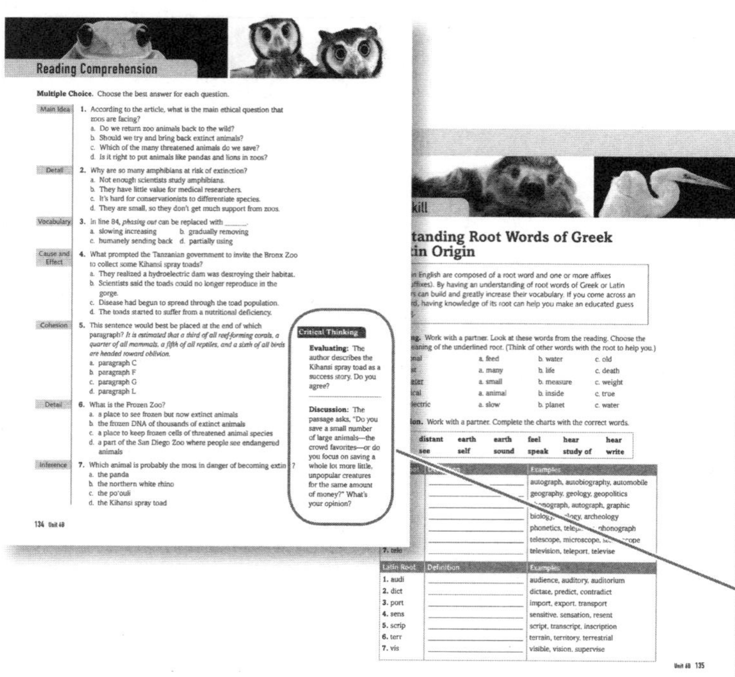

The Teacher's Guide has suggestions for the Reading Comprehension tasks in each chapter. Line numbers showing where the answers can be found in the passage are available in the Answer Key.

Critical Thinking challenge questions at the end of each Reading Comprehension page encourage students to evaluate the text critically, and support their opinions.

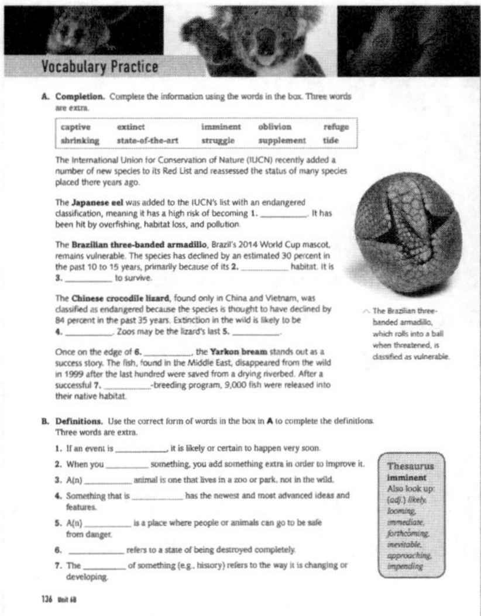

Vocabulary Building boxes highlight common collocations, affixes, and usage to develop learner independence. For example, **Word Link** boxes present common prefixes and suffixes to help students increase their vocabularies.

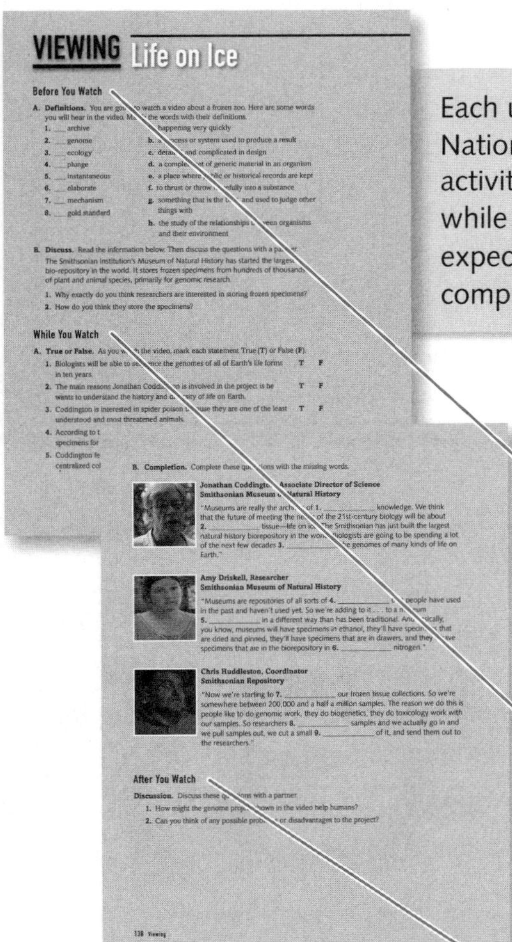

Each unit features a **Viewing** section based on a video from National Geographic that is related to the unit theme. Video activities provide additional comprehension and vocabulary practice while motivating learners to learn more about the unit topic. It is expected that the video will be played more than once, first for gist comprehension and then to let students focus on details.

A **Before You Watch** section activates students' background knowledge and familiarizes them with vocabulary they will encounter in the film. Students are often asked to predict information they think will be presented in the video.

The **While You Watch** section checks on the student's predictions, then shifts to a focus on details from the video. Sometimes this is organized as a word web summary; at other times students may have to sequence events or match statements with people in the video.

After You Watch usually contains several Critical Thinking questions that ask students to go beyond a literal interpretation of the video's contents. The activities vary, but students are challenged to synthesize information they have read and watched.

Aims and Principles

The *Reading Explorer* series aims to develop learners' skills in reading, vocabulary building, and critical thinking, using topics and visuals adapted from real-world National Geographic content.

A key principle of *Reading Explorer* is that today's learners need to be exposed to a wide variety of reading types. Information in the twenty-first century is increasingly conveyed in multimodal formats, that is, using a combination of text with graphics, diagrams, tables, photographs, and video. Exposure to the variety of formats in *Reading Explorer* will help learners to develop their visual literacy as well as their textual literacy.

Another principle of *Reading Explorer* is that fluent readers employ a variety of strategies for reading, which, in turn, is based on various purposes for reading. In other words, the reading process is often multipurpose.

With *Reading Explorer*, learners develop active learning strategies such as:

- Using their own background knowledge of the topic, and awareness of text types, in order to make predictions about a passage;
- Reading "top-down" to gain an overall idea of the purpose, type, and structure of a text;
- Processing "bottom-up" clues such as contextual information and word parts in order to comprehend unfamiliar vocabulary, and the meaning of cohesive markers such as pronoun references;
- Scanning a text quickly to locate specific information;
- Processing what is literally given in a text (literal comprehension) as well as what is implied or inferred by the writer (inferential comprehension);
- Recognizing relationships within a paragraph, or across a text, such as identifying cause and effect relationships, or the links between main and supporting ideas;
- Identifying what is factually true in a text, versus the writer's personal opinion.

An additional principle of the series is that reading is a ***multistage*** process. In particular, learners should be well prepared before they start to read a text and should later have an opportunity to reflect on what they have learned. This concept is known as the KWL technique.

Using this approach, students identify:

- What they *know* about the topic (i.e., their prior knowledge, or *schema*)
- What they *want* to know (i.e., their purpose for reading)
- What they *learned* (i.e., their comprehension of the reading)

With *Reading Explorer*, learners are also encouraged to go beyond the passage—and develop learner independence—by exploring the topic through the Classroom Audio CD/DVD Package and by exploring the topics online.

Teaching Tips

Preparing Learners to Read

How should teachers prepare for a unit?

Teachers should go through the unit themselves before a class, taking note of any questions students may have. The Teacher's Guide provides background information and resources to help answer students' questions. Relevant websites at the start of each unit provide opportunities to learn more, and students can be directed to them for further exploration. Take time to read the overview, answer keys, and detailed teaching notes on language, cultural background, and vocabulary. The Viewing section gives teaching suggestions on using the video effectively.

Why is it important to prepare learners before reading?

Reading is an interaction between what students already know about a topic and new material in a reading passage. They will understand and enjoy reading more if their background knowledge is drawn upon. Moreover, learners need a reason to read.

How should teachers use the Warm Up section?

Every *Reading Explorer* unit starts with a section called **Warm Up**. This helps students make connections between what they already *know*—the "K" part of the KWL approach—and the topics covered in the unit. Full-page photographs from National Geographic help raise students' interest in the unit theme, and discussion questions help students relate the reading topics to their own lives. The Teacher's Guide provides possible responses to these questions as well as additional challenge questions that encourage students to think about the overall theme of the unit.

How should teachers use the Before You Read section?

Before You Read is made up of two activities, A and B, and comes at the start of each lesson. Activity A often pre-teaches some key vocabulary and content that is essential to understanding the reading passage. These words (i.e., the support vocabulary) are presented in context and set in bold for emphasis. This support vocabulary appears later in the passage and is important for overall comprehension; however, it is not essential that students acquire (i.e., learn and remember) these words at this stage. More explanation about vocabulary, including the distinction between support and target vocabulary, is given on pages 14–16.

In Activity A, learners complete tasks such as using the bold words to label a photograph or map, matching definitions, answering questions, or completing a short paragraph. In the process, they build visual literacy skills by reading graphically presented information, such as captions, headers, map or graph keys, just as in magazines, in newspapers, and on the Internet.

Activity B provides a purpose for reading. For example, students should read the reading passage quickly to identify the main idea or make predictions about the content. Establishing what they want to learn is the "W" in KWL. It is important that *after* reading, teachers should take time to see what students have learned—"L" in KWL—from the passage.

What are the main previewing skills?

The main previewing skills are *skimming* (reading quickly for the main idea), *scanning* (reading quickly to find specific information), and *predicting* (using existing knowledge of a topic to anticipate the content of the passage). By reading quickly first, students are motivated to read more thoroughly later.

Building Learners' Reading Skills

What are the features of *Reading Explorer* texts?

Target vocabulary items are highlighted in red within the passage. These high-frequency words have been selected because they occur often in nonfiction reading. They are useful words that students should learn and remember. Target vocabulary is developed further in the vocabulary section within each unit and recycled throughout the series.

Teachers can teach target vocabulary in various ways. Some teachers may prefer to pre-teach these words before learners read the passage; others may prefer to wait until after learners have completed a first reading of the text, before they teach or elicit the meaning of the target words.

Titles and headers provide clues to the organization of a reading passage and the main ideas. Sometimes the pre-reading activities will draw special attention to them. Ask students about titles and headers after a first reading. Check whether they are able to put the headers into their own words. Often, paragraphs have one main idea expressed in the header.

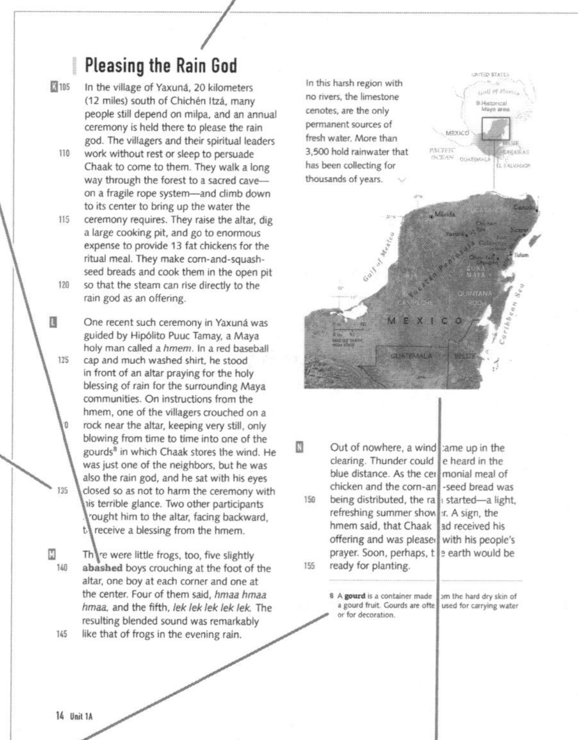

Pleasing the Rain God

K In the village of Yaxuná, 20 kilometers (12 miles) south of Chichén Itzá, many people still depend on milpa, and an annual ceremony is held there to please the rain god. The villagers and their spiritual leaders work without rest or sleep to persuade Chaak to come to them. They walk a long way through the forest to a sacred cave—on a fragile rope system—and climb down to its center to bring up the water the ceremony requires. They raise the altar, dig a large cooking pit, and go to enormous expense to provide 13 fat chickens for the ritual meal. They make corn-and-squash-seed breads and cook them in the open pit so that the steam can rise directly to the rain god as an offering.

L One recent such ceremony in Yaxuná was guided by Hipólito Puuc Tamay, a Maya holy man called a *hmem*. In a red baseball cap and much washed shirt, he stood in front of an altar praying for the holy blessing of rain for the surrounding Maya communities. On instructions from the hmem, one of the villagers crouched on a rock near the altar, keeping very still, only blowing from time to time into one of the gourds[8] in which Chaak stores the wind. He was just one of the neighbors, but he was also the rain god, and he sat with his eyes closed so as not to harm the ceremony with his terrible glance. Two other participants brought him to the altar, facing backward, to receive a blessing from the hmem.

M There were little frogs, too, five slightly **abashed** boys crouching at the foot of the altar, one boy at each corner and one at the center. Four of them said, *hmaa hmaa hmaa*, and the fifth, *lek lek lek lek lek*. The resulting blended sound was remarkably like that of frogs in the evening rain.

In this harsh region with no rivers, the limestone cenotes, are the only permanent sources of fresh water. More than 3,500 hold rainwater that has been collecting for thousands of years.

N Out of nowhere, a wind came up in the clearing. Thunder could be heard in the blue distance. As the ceremonial meal of chicken and the corn-and-seed bread was being distributed, the rain started—a light, refreshing summer shower. A sign, the hmem said, that Chaak had received his offering and was pleased with his people's prayer. Soon, perhaps, the earth would be ready for planting.

8 A **gourd** is a container made from the hard dry skin of a gourd fruit. Gourds are often used for carrying water or for decoration.

14 Unit 1A

Line numbers are provided every five lines in each reading passage. In class discussions, encourage students to use the line numbers when responding to comprehension questions. When students work in pairs, ask them to refer to the text using line numbers.

Footnote definitions for lower-frequency words (e.g., acronyms or technical terms) that are important for understanding the passage are provided at the bottom of the page.

Photographs, maps, graphics, and captions provide information that reinforces ideas from the reading passage. If students haven't been directed to use these resources in **Before You Read**, draw attention to them by asking questions that can be answered only with information found there. The Teacher's Guide provides suggestions for utilizing these resources to help promote visual literacy.

How can teachers promote reading fluency?

Reading fluency is the ability to read smoothly and effortlessly while understanding the ideas expressed in the text. To help learners achieve this goal, teachers can:

- Encourage learners to read chunks of text by phrases, rather than word by word.
- Discourage learners from "tracing" words with their fingers or subvocalizing (reading aloud) the words while reading, as these slow down the reading process.
- In subsequent readings of the passage, have students read quickly without stopping for a timed period such as two minutes. Then check how far the learners get each time.
- Play the audio recording of the passage from the CD, and have learners read the passage at the same speed.
- Recommend that learners avoid checking each unfamiliar word in a dictionary, particularly when they read a passage for the first time.

For further ideas on developing reading skills and fluency, see Anderson, N. J. (1999). *Exploring Second Language Reading: Issues and Strategies.* Boston: Heinle.

How should teachers check reading comprehension?

Reading comprehension activities check students' understanding and their ability to use specific reading skills. The comprehension section immediately follows each reading passage. Some teachers may prefer to have students attempt to answer the questions without referring back to the text. However, note that some comprehension questions specifically refer to paragraphs or lines in the text.

Additional reading comprehension questions can be found in the Online Workbook.

How can teachers promote reading skills?

The Reading Skill section explicitly teaches and practices one academic reading skill to enhance learner' reading comprehension. The section teaches a variety of reading skills, for example:

- Understanding Infographics (e.g., page 16 of the Student Book)
- Determining the Main Ideas of Paragraphs (e.g., page 38 of the Student Book)
- Scanning for Details (e.g., page 60 of the Student Book)
- Recognizing Literal vs. Figurative Language (e.g., page 81 of the Student Book)
- Distinguishing Main Ideas and Supporting Information (e.g., page 103 of the Student Book)
- Identifying Homonyms (e.g., page 125 of the Student Book)
- Understanding the Use of the Passive Voice (e.g., page 148 of the Student Book)

The Reading Skill section guides students in using several types of graphic organizers (Venn diagrams, T-charts, concept maps, flow charts, timelines, etc.). This gives students tools for organizing information in reading passages and helps them develop visual literacy skills.

How does *Reading Explorer* prepare students for standardized tests?

Reading Explorer has texts and question types similar to those used on international English exams. Each reading comprehension task has seven multiple-choice questions. Each question focuses on a particular skill, such as:

- Understanding the gist (overall theme) of the entire passage
- Choosing the main idea or the most appropriate title for the passage
- Identifying the main idea of smaller portions of text (e.g., a paragraph)
- Finding factual details (usually paraphrased from the text)
- Identifying the meaning of references in the text (e.g., pronoun references)
- Understanding the meaning of vocabulary in context (different from target or support vocabulary)
- Paraphrasing ideas

- Inferring someone's intention or opinion
- Detecting the author's purpose

The labels on the questions are also an effective teaching tool to familiarize students with their purposes and formats. The labels are explained in the glossary at the end of the Teacher's Guide.

Developing Learners' Vocabulary

What is *Reading Explorer*'s approach to language learning?

Reading Explorer aims to build the high-frequency vocabulary that learners need for academic and real-world success. The series presents words in context, and then follows with exercises that teach and recycle them. Vocabulary research has shown that both implicit and explicit instruction are important in developing vocabulary that students can retain and actively use. *Reading Explorer* provides teachers with both options.

What are the different types of vocabulary in *Reading Explorer*?

All components of *Reading Explorer*—reading texts, video, and audio—are carefully graded to build students' vocabulary. *Reading Explorer* categorizes vocabulary into the following types:

- **Target vocabulary:** These are high-frequency words in academic and non-fiction reading. Knowing them and their related forms will help students become effective and fluent readers. Target words are highlighted in red. Target vocabulary is practiced in the Vocabulary Practice section of each unit of the Student Book (e.g., page 17) and are recycled in the Viewing section.
- **Support vocabulary:** These words appear in bold in each unit's **Before You Read** section and are accompanied by photographs and graphics that help learners understand their meaning. They pre-teach vocabulary related to the topic of the reading passage.
- **Specialized or technical vocabulary:** These are footnoted within each passage, with definitions provided beneath the text.

What are some ways to teach vocabulary in context?

When learning another language, students need specific instructions in order to build vocabulary rapidly. Guessing the meaning of unknown or new words from context works best when students have already developed a sizeable core vocabulary. For this reason, teachers may choose to pre-teach the target vocabulary before learners approach the reading.

However, even elementary and intermediate students benefit from being taught skills for understanding new vocabulary in context. Here are some suggestions for building these skills:

- Draw attention to the target vocabulary highlighted in the passage. Have students pay attention to the surrounding words. Is the new word associated or collocated with other words?
- Decide on the new word's part of speech. How does it function in the sentence? Are there clues such as articles (*an*, *the*), adjectives, adverbs, or verb endings?
- Are some components of the word familiar? Look for clues to meaning in word roots, prefixes, and suffixes.
- Is the new word defined within the text? Sometimes a synonym is given nearby in the passage.

Teaching strategies for understanding words from context will promote better reading skills. Whenever possible, encourage students to work out meaning from context without interrupting the flow of their reading. In particular, suggest that students avoid using a dictionary to look up word meanings while reading, as this will slow them down and decrease their reading fluency. Several of the Reading Skill sections present strategies for using context to understand unfamiliar vocabulary.

The Teacher's Guide contains suggestions for presenting and practicing vocabulary for each unit. In addition, clarifications are provided for appropriate usage and cultural considerations of certain words.

How is target vocabulary practiced and reviewed?

After being presented in context in the main reading passage, target vocabulary items are subsequently recycled in several sections of the book:

1. The **Vocabulary Practice** pages in each unit focus on using the target vocabulary in various contexts. Sometimes students complete gaps in a reading with the key words. At other times, they manipulate target words or find appropriate definitions for them in context.

Knowing a word does not just involve knowing its spelling and meaning; it is also important that learners become aware of word structure, collocations, and usage. While much of the focus of the Vocabulary Practice page is on word meaning, the Vocabulary Building boxes supplement this by highlighting relevant word forms and associations. There are four types in Student Book 5:

Word Link: Students develop decoding strategies based on word parts such as roots, prefixes, and suffixes.

Word Partnerships: Common collocations and set phrases involving target vocabulary items are presented, so that learners can increase their vocabulary awareness through acquisition of lexical chunks.

Usage: Information is provided on common usage, such as the varied meanings of a word, and the distinction between formal and slang connotations.

Thesaurus: Students are encouraged to explore useful synonyms.

2. The **Viewing** section in each unit is based on a topic related to the unit theme. Many of the target vocabulary items are featured in the narration of the video, which has been carefully graded for language level. Expanded While You Watch and Before You Watch activities and Critical Thinking questions following the video give students an opportunity to use newly acquired vocabulary as they discuss the unit topic and relate it to their own ideas.

For more on using video in class, see pages 16–17 of this Teacher's Guide.

3. Additional vocabulary practice exercises can be found in the **Online Workbook**. These interactive and self-scoring activities review the target vocabulary from the Student Book and include question types such as multiple-choice, drag and drop, and sentence completion.

What role do dictionaries play in learning?

Although target vocabulary is presented and practiced in context in *Reading Explorer*, dictionaries still play an important role in learning vocabulary. Whichever dictionary you and your students decide to use, it is important to become familiar with its features and use it regularly. Some teachers find it helpful to bring a range of dictionaries to class and develop activities that require students to contrast and compare them.

What tips can teachers offer students in learning vocabulary?

As a teacher, you can help students become successful language learners by:

- Creating opportunities for vocabulary practice and making it fun
- Making your classroom "vocabulary rich" by placing notes and labels on walls and boards
- Creating flashcards and games (such as bingo and "hangman") as a way of reviewing recently learned vocabulary
- Including vocabulary in your assessment
- Teaching vocabulary acquisition strategies (such as learning key affixes and word roots)
- Using word webs, drawings, and other memory aids to help students remember words
- Requiring students to keep vocabulary notebooks and checking them often

- Promoting extensive reading by encouraging learners to read graded readers, such as the Footprint Reading Library, available at NGL.Cengage.com/footprint, or the Page Turners Reading Library, available at NGL.Cengage.com/pageturners.

For further ideas on teaching vocabulary, see Nation, I. S. P. (2008). *Teaching Vocabulary: Strategies and Techniques*. Boston: Heinle.

Using Video in Class

What are the features of the Viewing section?

The video features a theme related to the whole unit. It has three tasks:

- *Before You Watch:* This section prepares students for what they will be watching.
- *While You Watch:* This section requires students to complete a variety of activities about what they have watched. It recycles target vocabulary and tests students' understanding of the video.
- *After You Watch:* The questions in this section allow students to think critically about what they have learned in the unit, including ideas from the video, and to relate the unit to their own lives.

All video clips are on the **Classroom Audio CD/DVD Package**. The Online Workbook contains additional comprehension questions about the video.

Why teach video-viewing skills?

In daily life, nonfiction videos can be found on television, on the Internet, and in theaters as documentaries. Just as *Reading Explorer* provides a wide variety of authentic text and graphic material to build students' nonfiction reading skills, the series also builds viewing skills with videos from National Geographic. *Reading Explorer* promotes visual literacy so learners can competently use a wide range of modern media.

Videos differ from word texts in important ways. First, students are processing information by viewing and listening simultaneously. Visual images include information about the video's setting as well as nonverbal communication such as facial expressions and body movements. The soundtrack contains narration, conversations, music, and sound effects. Some contextual words may appear on screen in signs or as identification of people or settings. In addition, full English subtitles ("closed captions") are available as a teaching and learning option.

What are the stages of viewing?

Previewing prepares students for the video, engages their background knowledge about the topic, and creates interest in what they will watch. Effective previewing methods include:

- Brainstorming and discussing what the class already knows about the topic
- Using photographs and the video's title to predict the content
- Pre-teaching key vocabulary essential to understanding the video content

Viewing may occur multiple times and at different speeds while:

- Watching for gist comprehension or the main ideas from the film
- Watching and listening closely for detail
- Watching and listening for opinion and inference

Post-viewing activities include:

- Describing the main points and paying attention to the sequence of events and the individuals who speak
- Answering Critical Thinking questions that relate the video to the students' own lives or experiences

How should teachers use the videos to teach?

The narration on each video has been carefully graded to feature vocabulary and structures that are appropriate for students' proficiency levels. The location of the video section at the end of each unit ensures that students already bring background knowledge and target vocabulary to the viewing process.

Here are techniques for using video in class:

- Pause, rewind, or fast-forward the video to focus on key segments or events.
- Pause the video midway to allow students to predict what will happen next. Resume the video so students can check their predictions.
- Have students watch the video with the sound muted, to focus only on what they see. If this approach is used, follow-up discussion helps students share their ideas about the content of the video. Then play with sound for students to check their ideas.
- Have students watch without subtitles or sound and make predictions about what they will hear; then play with subtitles and sound for students to check their predictions.
- Have students follow the script (available on NGL.Cengage.com/readingexplorer) as they listen to the video to help in improving intonation, pitch, and stress. Stop and replay key phrases for students to repeat.
- Have students watch the video independently and complete the comprehension questions on the Online Workbook.

To extend viewing skills to speaking and writing skills, have students make a presentation or create a written report about a short video of their choice, using language they have learned from the Student Book and video narration.

Assessing Learners' Progress

How can learners' progress be assessed with *Reading Explorer*?

Ongoing assessment with *Reading Explorer* allows teachers to obtain feedback on students' progress in vocabulary, reading skills, and visual literacy. Ways that teachers can assess learners include:

- Reading comprehension questions that reflect current question formats on standardized English exams
- Vocabulary practice sections that check learners' understanding of recently acquired vocabulary
- Self-grading vocabulary activities and reading and viewing comprehension questions in the Online Workbook
- Assessment CD-ROM with ExamView® so teachers can quickly create customized tests

The ExamView® software provided with *Reading Explorer* contains banks of questions on readings and vocabulary for each unit. The questions mirror many of the types and formats of questions used in the Student Book. With ExamView®, teachers can create and customize exams quickly and easily.

The ExamView® component provides the following for each unit of *Reading Explorer*:

- An additional reading passage related to the unit topic, with comprehension questions
- A bank of additional questions relating to the target vocabulary of the unit

The questions cover a variety of task types, including multiple choice, true or false, and completion. The reading comprehension questions focus on the same range of reading skills that are highlighted in the Student Book, for example, understanding main ideas, details, and inferences, identifying references, and understanding vocabulary from context.

Name: ______________________ Class: ______________

Reading Explorer: Reading Summary Worksheet

Unit: ______________ Reading title: ______________________

A. What is the reading passage mostly about?

____

B. What places are mentioned in the reading?

____

____

C. In a few words, give the topic or main idea of each paragraph:

____

____

____

____

____

____

D. Describe one of the photos or graphics in the reading. Did it give you an example of something in the text or provide additional information? Explain.

____

____

E. List the ten words highlighted in the text. Write a sentence or definition for each.

1. ______________ ______________________
2. ______________ ______________________
3. ______________ ______________________
4. ______________ ______________________
5. ______________ ______________________
6. ______________ ______________________
7. ______________ ______________________
8. ______________ ______________________
9. ______________ ______________________
10. ______________ ______________________

F. Make a sentence using one of the words in the footnotes.

____

G. What are two or three things that you learned from this reading?

____

____

Name: ______________________________ Class: ______________

Reading Explorer: Video Summary Worksheet

Unit: ______________ Video title: ______________________________

A. Note the people, locations, and events that you see in the video.

____

____

____

____

B. In a few words, give the main idea of the video.

____

____

C. Answer these questions about the video.

Where was it filmed? Give the name of the location(s) and continent(s):

____

Who are the people in the video (if any)? What are their jobs?

____

____

What was the main *purpose* of the video? For example, to give information, to entertain, or to persuade you to change your mind about something.

____

____

D. Were there words or phrases in the video that were new to you? Note them here, with a definition or sample sentence.

____

____

____

E. What are two or three things that you learned from the video?

____

____

____

F. If *you* could film this video, what would you do differently?

____

____

____

Unit 1 Collapse

Unit Introduction

This unit focuses on ancient civilizations. Students will read about new information on the beliefs of the ancient and modern Maya and then learn about the fall of the city of Angkor in Cambodia.

Key Words for Internet Research:
Maya, Holtún cenote, archeology, Yucatán, Chichén Itzá, Angkor, Angkor Wat, Greater Angkor Project, Bernard-Philippe Groslier, cultural collapse, Khmer Empire

For More Information:
http://ngm-beta.nationalgeographic.com/archive/maya-sacred-cenotes/

Warm Up

Answer Key

1. Answers will vary. Possibilities include: Romans, Maya, Aztecs, Incans.
2. Possibilities include: natural disasters, depletion of natural resources, war with other civilizations. **3.** Answers will vary.

Teaching Notes

Note that the Warm Up introduces the main idea of the unit and helps to activate the students' background knowledge of the topic(s). Asking students about the photograph emphasizes the importance of infographics as a way of conveying information. Moreover, this section focuses the class on the unit topic and gives students a chance to make contributions from their different backgrounds.

Have students look at the photo and read the caption. Ask them:

- **What are moai?** They are statues of humans, at least of their heads, made by the people on Easter Island.
- **Why do you think the Rapa Nui made them?** Perhaps to honor ancestors, chiefs, or other important people, but no one really knows.
- **When were these made?** Between the 10th and the 16th century, during the height of the Rapa Nui society.
- **Where is Easter Island?** It's 2,300 miles (3,700 kilometers) west of South America and 1,100 miles (1,770 kilometers) from the nearest neighboring island.
- **What are moai made out of?** Volcanic rock.

Lesson 1A Secrets of the Maya

Lesson Overview

Target Vocabulary: abashed, astonished, demise, flourish, grueling, inspect, penetrate, plunge, sacrifices, transparent

Reading Passage Summary: The passage covers recent discoveries by archeologists about the practices of the ancient Maya people. Archeologists have learned that caves, or cenotes, in Mexico could act like sundials, and helped the Maya create their incredibly accurate calendars. The cenotes were also part of their religious beliefs, and are linked to their planting cycles.

Answer Key

Before You Read

A. 1. Answers will vary. Possibilities include: archeologist, geologist, cave explorer.
2. Answers will vary. Possibilities include: religion, culture, mineral wealth, fresh water; The light shining down may signify time, God, seasons.
B. 1. ancient Mayan city (line 2); **2.** the God of life-giving rain and ruler of cenotes and caves (line 42 and line 66); **3.** a combination of corn, beans, and squash that constitutes their basic source of protein (lines 84–86); **4.** a Maya holy man (lines 123–124)

Reading Comprehension

1. b (lines 3–7); **2.** c (line 17); **3.** a (lines 25–34); **4.** a (lines 64–73); **5.** c (lines 86–87); **6.** d (lines 94–101); **7.** d

Reading Skill

A. 1. b; **2.** d; **3.** c; **4.** a
B. 1. NG; **2.** F; **3.** F; **4.** T; **5.** NG; **6.** F

Vocabulary Practice

A. 1. flourished; **2.** grueling; **3.** inspected; **4.** penetrate; **5.** demise
B. 1. b; **2.** a; **3.** b; **4.** a; **5.** b

Teaching Notes

Before You Read

A. Discussion: Students will need to read the information under the photo before they can answer the discussion questions. Tell students to give reasons for their ideas.

B. Scanning: Review what scanning is and strategies for scanning for specific information [looking for capital letters, looking for different formatting such as the use of italics]. Students individually complete the task and then compare answers with a partner.

Reading Comprehension

Have students read the entire passage silently and answer the comprehension questions. Check answers as a class, asking students to give evidence for their answers using line numbers from the reading passage.

As you review students' answers, point out how detail questions are different from those that ask about the main idea. For detail questions like 2 (NOT questions), point out that students have to confirm that the men are investigating three things, but not the fourth. It functions almost like four true/false questions.

Comprehension questions often include an item about the author's purpose. Sometimes the question is about the purpose of the entire passage, and sometimes it is about specific paragraphs as it is in question 7. In answering figurative language questions, such as 3, you may want to review common figurative language forms (i.e., similes and metaphors) so students know how to identify comparisons.

Critical Thinking

Inferring: The reading passage goes on to discuss the difficulty of farming in this area—the fact that successful farming requires a particular sequence of events and that droughts can be catastrophic. Luis Un Ken talks about a recent rain as he wipes the sweat off his face. Mentioning that he is an optimist previews the discussion of the challenges of life in this area, including the importance of rain.

Discussion: Students should support their opinions with examples or details, especially information from the reading passage.

Reading Skill

A. Matching: Have students identify the kind of information presented in the infographic. [This infographic includes photos, diagrams, text, illustrations, and captions.]

Have students spend a few minutes just looking at the original infographic to notice the kind of information they see presented. The next step is to determine what kind of information they need to complete activity A. If they have completed a visual survey of the infographic, they should be able to locate the details more successfully.

B. True or False: In activity B, students identify information that is not given in the infographic, as well as what statements are true or false. Have students compare answers before you check answers as a class. Items 1 and 5 address information that is not given in the infographic. As with all true/false questions, suggest students identify key words in each statement that they can scan for in the infographic. For example, students might identify *enter, cenote,* and *jump* in the first item. If they scan the infographic, they won't find *enter* and *jump* linked to *cenote.*

Vocabulary Practice

A. Completion: Have students work in pairs to look at the passage and identify the parts of speech of the words in the box. Then have them list other forms of these words as they will need to use the correct form in activity A. As you check answers, ask students to explain how they knew which form of the word to use.

Students will have to change the word form in 1 and 3. Elicit how students know which form to use (e.g., in 1, they will need to use simple past as the entire paragraph is in the past).

B. Words in Context: Have students complete the sentences by choosing the correct answers. Students can check their understanding of the meaning of the words by referring to the passage and substituting the answers in B.

Word Partnership

Point out that *sacrifice* can be either a noun or a verb. Elicit the meanings of the words in bold. Ask students to give examples of each of the phrases in the box.

Lesson 1B The Collapse of Angkor

Lesson Overview

Target Vocabulary: assume, channels, disperse, doomed, ingenuity, internal, mechanism, regime, scarce, subsequent

Reading Passage Summary: The passage covers possible reasons for the downfall of the Khmer city of Angkor. These reasons include invaders, changes in religion, a shift to maritime trade, and droughts that impacted the waterways of the kingdom.

Answer Key

Before You Read

A. Jayavarman II, Angkor, Theravada Buddhism, 1400s

B. Answers will vary. Possible answers include: foreign invaders, changes in religion, natural disasters.

Reading Comprehension

1. a; **2.** c; **3.** c; **4.** d; **5.** d; **6.** d (lines 137–143); **7.** b

Reading Skill
A. 1. e; **2.** b; **3.** d; **4.** c; **5.** a
B. Supporting evidence for each argument in part A includes: **1.** Historians deduced that Angkor had been looted (lines 24–27); **2.** No extra evidence given; **3.** Economic reasons (lines 70–76); **4.** No extra evidence given; **5.** Europe experienced the Little Ice Age (lines 140–143).

Vocabulary Practice
A. 1. dispersing; **2.** channels; **3.** scarce; **4.** internal; **5.** mechanism
B. 1. a; **2.** b; **3.** b; **4.** b; **5.** a

Teaching Notes

Before You Read

Have students read the title and caption. Then direct students' attention to the timeline on the left of the photo. Check comprehension by asking questions: *Where is the beginning of the timeline? What happened in 802–850 A.D.? How many years did Angkor exist? What were the names of neighboring kingdoms?*

A. Completion: Students will need to use the information in the timeline and in the caption below the photo to complete the activity.

B. Skimming and Predicting: Ask students where important information about main ideas is usually found. Elicit that the first and last paragraphs of a passage as well as the first and last sentences of individual paragraphs often contain important information. Give students one minute to skim page 19. Elicit some predictions from the class.

Reading Comprehension

Before students complete this exercise, have them look at their predictions to check how accurate they were.

Have students read the entire passage silently and answer the comprehension questions. Check answers as a class, asking students to give evidence for their answers using line numbers from the reading passage.

The first question asks about the purpose of the article as a whole. Ask students where they found this answer. Remind students that main ideas, or the purpose of an entire text, are often located at the beginning and at the end of a passage. In question 2, students will again have to confirm that three answers are correct and one is incorrect.

Critical Thinking

Evaluating: This is a two-part exercise. Students first have to identify the challenges. Put students in pairs or small groups to answer the first question. You may want to elicit these challenges and write them on the board before students discuss the second question. This will help them generate more ideas. Possible answers include: climate change, failing waterways, shift of power.

Discussion: Students should support their opinions with examples or details, especially information from the reading passage. Encourage them to identify aspects of culture or national character that might be represented by the place or monument they chose.

Reading Skill

Go over the information in the box. Make sure students understand the meaning of any unfamiliar words. Elicit ways in which students can distinguish between facts and opinions. Students should identify that some adjectives (e.g., *beautiful, important, surprising*) convey opinions, as do verbs such as *believe, think, assume, claim, deduce,* and the use of modals or adverbs (e.g., *may, might, could have, maybe*).

A. Analyzing: Have students work individually to match the arguments with the supporting evidence. Check answers as a class.

B. Evaluating: Give students a few minutes to scan the article again and search for other evidence mentioned in the article. Note that not all the arguments are supported by other evidence.

Vocabulary Practice

A. Definitions: First, have students read the passage individually, paying attention to the words in red. Then have them use context to match the words to their definitions.

B. Words in Context: Have students complete the sentences by choosing the correct answers. Suggest students find the words in the passage to get more context for the words.

Word Link

Elicit the meanings of the words in italics. Ask students how each word is related to the root meaning "rule."

VIEWING: Temples in the Jungle

Video Summary: Angkor was the capital of the Khmer civilization that once controlled more than half of Asia. In the 15th century, however, the Khmer's story came to an end following poor harvests and attacks by the kingdom of Siam. The people dispersed, and the city was consumed by jungle.

Answer Key

Before You Watch

A. 1. T; **2.** F; **3.** F; **4.** T; **5.** T

B. a. ingenious; **b.** intrinsic; **c.** sophisticated; **d.** pieced together; **e.** fled

While You Watch

A. The following should be checked: the size of Angkor; when the Khmer fled Angkor; how long it took to build Angkor Wat; attacks on Angkor; a visit by a French naturalist.

B. 1. When Henri Mouhot visited the ruins of Angkor, he **drew** pictures of the city.; **2.** Angkor Wat served as a **shrine**, **an observatory**, and a funerary temple.; **3.** After the Chams attacked, Angkor Wat was **rebuilt** and the king built Angkor Thom.; **4.** A huge battle in the **15th** century almost destroyed the Khmer people.

After You Watch

1. and **2.** Answers will vary.

Teaching Notes

Before You Watch

For suggestions on building students' viewing skills, see page 16.

A. Have students complete the activity in groups or pairs without looking back at the reading from Lesson 1B to see how much they can remember. Note that sentence 2 is false as Angkor Wat was originally built in honor of a *Hindu* god. Sentence 3 is also incorrect as the first Europeans in Angkor found a dying city.

B. Have students work individually to match the words with their definitions before checking answers together. Note that *fled* is the past form of the verb *flee*.

While You Watch

Follow these steps:

1. Students watch the video through once, checking the topics in activity A that are mentioned in the video. Check answers as a class.
2. Before playing the video a second time, ask students to try to answer the While You Watch questions in activity B from memory. Play the video a second time, pausing the video after key sections so that students can complete the sentences.
3. After they've watched the video a second time, students check answers with a partner.
4. If necessary, play the video through a third time. Then check answers as a class.

After You Watch

Students discuss the questions in pairs. Call on students to share their ideas with the class.

Unit 2

Beyond Earth

Unit Introduction

This unit focuses on our quest to learn about space. Students will read about a very powerful telescope in the Chilean desert, and then learn about how scientists try to detect the existence of other planets in our galaxy and beyond.

Key Words for Internet Research:
cosmic dawn, ALMA, Atacama Desert, Doppler technique, dwarf stars, exoplanet

For More Information:
http://www.nationalgeographic.com/cosmic-dawn
http://www.nationalgeographic.com/astrobiology

Warm Up

Answer Key

1. Answers will vary. Possibilities include: telescopes, space probes, satellites, space exploration. **2.** Answers will vary. Possibilities include: calendars, navigation, physics.
3. Answers will vary. He probably meant that if people are unsure about something, they will try to invent something to find the answer.

Teaching Notes

Have students look at the photo and read the caption. Ask them:

- **What is a galaxy?** A galaxy is a large system made up of stars, planets, dark matter, and gas and dust. There are more than 170 billion galaxies in the universe. The Earth is part of the Milky Way Galaxy.
- **What is the Hubble telescope?** The Hubble Space Telescope is a telescope that orbits the Earth. It was launched in 1990.
- **Why might the Hubble Telescope work better than telescopes on land?** It's above the atmosphere, which distorts and blocks light.
- **Where is the ALMA Telescope?** It's in the Atacama Desert in Chile. Students will read more about this in Lesson A.
- **What is a light-year?** A light-year measures distance in space. One light-year is how far light will travel in one Earth year. Light travels at an incredible 300,000 kilometers (186,000 miles) per second. A light year is about 9.5 trillion kilometers (5.88 trillion miles). The nearest star to our Sun is approximately four light years away.

Lesson 2A Cosmic Dawn

Lesson Overview

Target Vocabulary: accompany, companion, coordinate, distorted, emit, interpret, interrupt, in operation, position (*v.*), set up

Reading Passage Summary: The passage talks about the ALMA telescope in Chile, explaining how and why it was built, its advantages over other modern telescopes, and some of the scientific discoveries it has helped make.

Answer Key

Before You Read

A. 1. T; **2.** F; **3.** T; **4.** F

B. Answers will vary. Possibilities include: **a.** what telescopes do/looking at the sky; **b.** the best place for a telescope/Atacama Desert; **c.** putting the array together; **d.** what we've learned from ALMA/other galaxies

Reading Comprehension

1. b (line 15); **2.** b; **3.** a (lines 78–80; **4.** d; **5.** b; **6.** d; **7.** a (lines 138–149)

Reading Skill

A. 1. b; **2.** b; **3.** a

B. 1. b; **2.** a; **3.** b; **4.** a; **5.** b; **6.** b; **7.** b; **8.** b

Vocabulary Practice

A. 1. positioned; **2.** set up; **3.** operation; **4.** emit; **5.** distort

B. 1. b; **2.** a; **3.** a; **4.** b; **5.** a

Teaching Notes

Before You Read

A. True or False: Students will need to read the information under the photo as well as in the photo itself before they can answer the T/F questions.

B. Skimming and Predicting: Review what skimming is [reading quickly to get the gist or main idea of a passage]. Point out that skimming and predicting helps students do two things: activate background knowledge and anticipate content. Both strategies will help them understand and remember information better. Students individually complete the task and then compare answers with a partner.

Reading Comprehension

Have students read the entire passage silently and answer the comprehension questions. Check answers as a class, asking students to give evidence for their answers using line numbers from the reading passage.

Question 2 asks about the purpose of a particular paragraph. All of the answers are addressed in the paragraph, but students need to determine the main purpose of the text. Note that in question 7, option *a* is the correct choice as ALMA had already done all these things before the installation was officially opened.

Critical Thinking

Inferring: The passage mentions the cooperative effort in paragraph G on page 32. Ask students to skim the text to find examples of challenges in the project itself, and then have them discuss how those challenges would be amplified or solved through international cooperation.

Discussion: Students should support their opinions with details from the reading passage related to what makes a location good for this project.

Reading Skill

A. Multiple Choice: For part A, suggest students identify the key words in each answer option (e.g., *history, types, locate, portable arrays, ideal spot, challenges*). As students reread the paragraphs, they should pay attention to terms and ideas related to these key words.

B. Matching: In Part B may be easier for students because the paragraph options are usually far apart in the passage, and because the subheadings provide clues. For example, question 1 is about discoveries, and the subheading before paragraph K is *Early Discoveries.* In question 6, the paragraphs are closer together and in the same section, but the first sentence of each paragraph identifies different time spans. You may want to suggest students answer the questions based on their memory of the text, and then go back and reread to confirm their answers.

Vocabulary Practice

A. Completion: Students will have to change word forms to complete this activity. *Position* and *set up*, in particular, require manipulation as they are both gerunds following prepositions in the passage and are in participle form as part of passive sentences in this exercise. Students may know the word *operation* when used to mean a surgery, but may not know this meaning, being in the process of working.

B. Words in Context: Have students use their knowledge of word parts to help with this task. For example, *companion* and *accompany* have the same root—*com* + *panis,* which means "with bread." A companion is someone you would share bread with. Both *interpret* and *interrupt* use the prefix *inter-* which means "between" or "among." The word *coordinate* uses the prefix *co-*, meaning "with" or "together."

Word Link

To help students expand their vocabularies, elicit the noun forms for these verbs, which will involve adding the suffix *-ission* to each.

Lesson 2B Planet Hunters: Are We Alone?

Lesson Overview

Target Vocabulary: comment, composition, exert, hence, inconspicuous, nucleus, orient, scope, steady, to date

Reading Passage Summary: The passage covers our search for other worlds in the universe, including the ways that scientists can discern planets that might be similar to the Earth and so be habitable. It also addresses the challenges of detecting life on other planets, especially as it may be unlike life as we know it on Earth.

Answer Key

Before You Read

A. 1. They know its size, mass, and distance from its sun.; It's the largest exoplanet they have found.; **2.** Answers will vary. An exoplanet is a planet orbiting a star other than the sun. One reason for hunting for them is that some may have conditions suitable for life. The main challenges involve the distances these planets are from the Earth, and their relatively small size and brightness compared to stars.
B. 1. the first and third questions; **2.** Answers will vary.

Reading Comprehension

1. c; **2.** a (lines 7–8); **3.** d; **4.** c;
5. b (lines 104–110); **6.** a (lines 114–120); **7.** c

Reading Skill

A. 1. e; **2.** c; **3.** h; **4.** a; **5.** f; **6.** g; **7.** b; **8.** d

Vocabulary Practice

A. 1. composition; **2**. To date; **3.** exerted;
4. conspicuous; **5.** Hence; **6.** commented;
7. scope
B. 1. nucleus; **2.** scope; **3.** oriented; **4.** comment;
5. exert; **6.** steadily; **7.** to date; **8.** conspicuous;
9. composition; **10.** hence

Teaching Notes

Before You Read

A. Discussion: Students will need to read the information under the photo before they can answer the discussion questions. For greater challenge, ask students to list five things they know about CT Cha b. Elicit what the prefix *exo* means (outside).

B. Skimming and Predicting: Elicit how students chose the questions they did in 1 (i.e., what information did they notice in their skimming that helped their decision). Students individually complete the task and then compare answers with a partner.

Reading Comprehension

Have students read the entire passage silently and answer the comprehension questions. Check answers as a class, asking students to give evidence for their answers using line numbers from the reading passage.

This is the first time students have seen the word *gist* as part of the reading comprehension questions. Elicit what *gist* means (the general idea). Ask how they can determine gist (skimming, attention to headings, introduction, and conclusion).

In this exercise, the questions about gist, inference, and cohesion will likely be more difficult than the detail questions. In question 1, both *b* and *c* are plausible answers. Focus on why *c* is a better answer than *b* (*b* mentions only "intelligent life" whereas the article discusses any forms of life). In 6, students can rule out *c* because methane, ozone ,and oxygen do not make the red edge—chlorophyll-containing plants do. This fact also rules out *b*. Paragraph L specifically states that life could have evolved differently on other planets at the same time. This leaves *a* as the correct answer.

Critical Thinking

Inferring: The conclusion is probably the best source of information in making this inference. The author clearly believes that Earthlike exoplanets will be found as he/she compares this hunt to explorations that humans have already done. The question is whether it will be in the "near future." The citing of the difficulty of these explorations suggests that it might not be very soon.

Discussion: Students should support their opinions with examples or details, especially information from the reading passage. Their answers will vary depending on a variety of factors, including religious views, tastes in movies, and interest in science.

Reading Skill

Matching: After students have read the information in the skill box, have them read the sentence parts in the exercise. Many students may be able to complete this task using what they remember from the passage and their own understanding of the relationship between ideas. For example, in 1, if students understand that an orbit of a sun takes one year, *e* is the obvious completion. Some students may find it helpful to scan the reading for the specific ideas and underline connectors that show a cause/effect relationship. Questions 5, 6, and 7 all deal with red edges. Students will need to look at paragraphs J–L to determine these relationships.

Vocabulary Practice

A. Completion: Students complete a reading passage by choosing between two words. Have students identify the parts of speech needed for each completion. Point out that *hence* and *to date* are adverbs as well as connecting words, and that other adverbs can be used in a similar way. The transition words may pose the greatest difficulty for students in this exercise.

B. Definitions: Suggest students identify what part of speech is needed in each definition. For this task, they do not have to change word forms.

Word Link

Point out that they worked with this word part in Lesson A (*companion, accompany*). Have students add other forms to each word family (e.g., *compose, composition, composed, composure*).

VIEWING: Comet Watchers

Video Summary: Scientists and amateurs gather at Mauna Kea, the Earth's highest volcano, to view Halley's Comet. Mauna Kea is a particularly good spot for viewing the comet because it reaches nearly halfway to outer space and it has special telescopes that allow researchers to take photographs.

Answer Key

Before You Watch

1. The comet was last here in 1986, so only those who were alive then and old enough could have seen it. **2.** It will next be seen in 2061 or 2062. **3.** People see "shooting stars" or comets/asteroids fairly frequently. It's easier if you have a telescope and if you know when and where one is expected.

While You Watch

A. 1, how the early explorers used the stars to navigate; 2, advantages of Mauna Kea as a viewing point; 3, the comet's age and frequency of appearance; 4, viewing the comet with telescopes; 5, viewing the comet using spacecraft
B. 1. volcano; **2.** pollution; **3.** winds; **4.** tail; **5.** camera; **6.** temperatures; **7.** spacecraft; **8.** dust

After You Watch

Answers will vary.

Teaching Notes

Before You Watch

For suggestions on building students' viewing skills, see page 16.

This video is mainly about Halley's Comet and how we can learn more about it. Some comet watchers just want to see a once-in-a-lifetime phenomenon, but astronomers want to learn as much as they can about it, including its size, composition, and density. The comet, like other features of the night sky, are a source of beauty that help us understand more about ourselves and the world.

While You Watch

Follow these steps:

1. Students watch the video through once, bearing in mind the answers they gave in Before You watch. Students can also complete the sequencing activity. Check answers as a class. Note that early explorers are mentioned right at the start of the video, so ensure students are paying attention.
2. Before playing the video a second time, ask students to try to answer the While You Watch questions in part B. You may want to pause the video after sections so that students can fill in the words.
3. After they've watched the video a second time, students check answers with a partner.
4. If necessary, play the video through a third time. Then check answers as a class.

After You Watch

Students discuss the questions in pairs. Call on students to share their ideas with the class. Dale Cruikshank probably means that studying stars and their planets allows us to understand more about how unique, or otherwise, life on Earth really is.

Unit 3 Health and Genes

Unit Introduction

This unit focuses on the role of genetics in health problems. Students will read about factors leading to heart diesease and researchers' attempts to identify genes that may contribute to it. Then students learn about allergies and possible reasons for why they are increasing.

Key Words for Internet Research:
heart disease, dysfunctional MEF2A, cholesterol, statins, allergies, common allergens, asthma, the Hygiene Hypothesis

For More Information:
http://ngm-beta.nationalgeographic.com/archive/misery-for-all-seasons-allergies-a-modern-epidemic
http://ngm-beta.nationalgeographic.com/archive/mending-broken-hearts

Warm Up

Answer Key

1. Answers will vary. Possibilities include: heart disease, cancer, stroke, diabetes, HIV/AIDS.
2. Answers will vary. Possibilities include: the body's reaction to allergens such as dust, pollen, seafood, peanuts. **3.** Answers will vary. Students will probably mention diseases that have environmental components such as cancer, lung disease, heart disease, diabetes, and asthma.

Teaching Notes

Before students open their books, ask them what things are important in maintaining good health. Write their ideas on the board.

Have students look at the photo and read the caption. Ask them:

- **What is a factor?** Something that plays a role in causing something else.
- **What is a healthy diet?** A healthy diet includes a lot of fruits and vegetables, lean protein, whole grains, and good fats like olive oil. It is low in fat, sugar, and processed foods.
- **What kind of exercise is good for your health?** Any exercise is good, but aerobic exercise like walking, running, swimming, and bicycling has proven beneficial effects on health.
- **What diseases have a genetic link?** There are many: Tay-Sachs, sickle cell anemia, some forms of cancer, Alzheimer's, cystic fibrosis, muscular dystrophy, Parkinson's, Huntington's. Some diseases are inherited, as genes are passed down from parents to children. Sometimes the faulty gene occurs spontaneously.

Lesson 3A Mending Broken Hearts

Lesson Overview

Target Vocabulary: component, compound, exacerbate, mutate, principal, proportion, stress, submit, susceptible, volume

Reading Passage Summary: The passage discusses heart disease and how new discoveries about genetic triggers may enable us to identify and anticipate such problems before they start.

Answer Key

Before You Read

A. 1. Tobacco smoking, physical activity, and poor diet; **2.** Answers may vary. Possible answer: High level of cholesterol creates plaque, which in turn causes atherosclerosis, or the narrowing of arteries, and this leads to a heart attack.
B. b

Reading Comprehension

1. a; **2.** a (lines 45–48); **3.** c; **4.** d (line 75); **5.** c (lines 79-83);**6.** a (lines 103–105); **7.** b

Reading Skill

1. one percent, line 59; **2.** genetic susceptibility to disease by adding up the number of risky variables, lines 68–70; **3.** his wife overheard a doctor describing a study, lines 18–21; **4.** How much blood is flowing through an artery, lines 88–92; **5.** DNA samples from patients who enter hospitals with atherosclerosis, lines 54–55; **6.** Cleveland Clinic, lines 23–26; **7.** his friend had nitroglycerin, line 9; **8.** elevated cholesterol, lines 96–98

Vocabulary Practice

A. 1. submitting; **2.** impeding; **3.** volume; **4.** proportions; **5.** compounded; **6.** stress; **7.** exacerbate; **8.** susceptible
B. 1. impede; **2.** stress; **3.** mutate; **4.** volume; **5.** proportion; **6.** susceptible; **7.** principal; **8.** submit

Teaching Notes

Before You Read

A. Discussion: The information on the photo uses some medical vocabulary that may be unfamiliar to students. The key terms below the photo explain the medical terminology. Give students time to read the information a couple of times.

B. Skimming and Predicting: Although the reading touches on eating habits and methods to control heart disease, most of the passage is about genetic factors.

Reading Comprehension

Discuss the main idea of the passage before going over the answers. Students should have confirmed their predictions after reading the passage. For more practice with understanding the main idea, have students work in pairs to write one sentence that sums up the entire passage. Have volunteers put their sentences on the board for the class to analyze.

Question 3 may be difficult for students as substituting all of the answers in the original sentence may sound plausible. Students will need to refer to the previous paragraph which says that Ellis suspects that dozens of genes contribute to a predisposition to heart disease. This suggests that they are still looking for such genes.

In question 6, students should be able to rule out *b* and *d* as they are not mentioned with statins in particular. In paragraph M, students learn that statins have side effects including muscle aches, and that patients should have tests to check liver function. This suggests that liver function may be affected.

If students have difficulty with question 7, direct them to paragraphs 2 and 4 on page 58, both of which point out that the "clogged-pipes" model has problems.

Critical Thinking

Analyzing: Students can scan the paragraphs for the words *gene* and *genetic* to find evidence (paragraphs A, D, E, G, H, I, L, N).

Discussion: Elicit examples of disease-causing genes that have been identified, and how that has impacted the patients involved (e.g., Angelina Jolie had a mastectomy, some parents choose to discontinue pregnancies when the fetus has a devastating disease, people with the genes for Huntington's, early-onset Alzheimer's, and Parkinson's face difficult futures). Students may want to include quality of life issues in their discussion.

Reading Skill

Scanning: The easiest information to scan for is dates and names. Other content can be more elusive. Suggest students underline or highlight key words in each question in the activity. Then have them work in pairs to generate a list of synonyms or other words in the same family. For example, a key word in question 1 is *percentage,* so students can scan for numbers, the percent symbol, or the word *percent.*

These items are not in the order as they appear in the passage. Students will be more efficient if they have identified the key words in all items before they begin scanning the passage as a whole.

Vocabulary Practice

A. Completion: All the words in this exercise have the same part of speech as in the passage except for *susceptible,* which appears as *susceptibility* in the reading. Students can use their knowledge of word parts to help with this task and also with part B [*sub* = under, *mit* = send or throw, *com* = together, *-ible* = able to be, *im* = not, *pede* = foot].

B. Definitions: In question 3, students will have to change a noun form to a verb (*mutation – mutate*). Otherwise, they can use the same part of speech as in part A. In 1 and 8, students will use the base form rather than the present participle (*-ing*).

Usage

Students will likely be familiar with *compound nouns* and *compound adjectives.* Elicit some examples from the class and use these to illustrate the meaning of *compound* as an adjective to mean "made of two or more parts."

Lesson 3B The War on Allergies

Lesson Overview

Target Vocabulary: component, confer, culprit, federal, legislation, miserable, register, set off, suppress, tolerate

Reading Passage Summary: In this passage, students learn about the growing epidemic of allergies—what they are, how they develop, and the factors that contribute. Such factors include genetics, diet, the use of antibiotics, pollutants, and too much cleanliness (or insufficient exposure to microbes).

Answer Key

Before You Read

A. 1. Pollen causes hay fever allergies, producing sneezing; watery, red eyes; and often difficulty breathing. **2.** Answers will vary. Possibilities include: dust, mold, nuts, seafood, poison ivy. They may get hives and have trouble breathing.
B. 1. 1, b; **2.** 24, a; **3.** 52, e; **4.** 122, c

Reading Comprehension

1. d; **2.** c; **3.** c (lines 40–42); **4.** a;
5. a (lines 59–60); **6.** b (lines 88–91); **7.** c

Reading Skill
1. asthmatic; **2.** rapid; **3.** diet; **4.** processed; **5.** vegetables, antioxidants, minerals; **6.** bacteria; **7.** overuse; **8.** diesel; **9.** pollutants; **10.** Hygiene; **11.** dirt/microbes; **12.** insulation; **13.** mold and dust

Vocabulary Practice
A. 1. miserable; **2.** culprit; **3.** confer; **4.** suppress; **5.** tolerates; **6.** legislation; **7.** federal; **8.** set off
B. 1. miserable; **2.** components; **3.** suppressed; **4.** registers; **5.** confer

Teaching Notes

Before You Read

Have students look at the photo. Ask when flowers are usually in bloom. Ask if anyone in the class has allergies/hay fever when flowers are blooming. Then have students look at the other visuals that accompany the text. Ask them to predict topics using the photos and diagrams.

A. Discussion: Make sure students understand the vocabulary in the caption (e.g., *grain, invader, trigger, overactive*).

B. Scanning and Predicting: Encourage students to scan the text for the bold, capitalized fonts, which will help them locate the start of each section.

Reading Comprehension

Have students read the entire passage silently and answer the comprehension questions. Check answers as a class, asking students to give evidence for their answers using line numbers from the reading passage.

Suggest students review their answers to part B of Before You Read as they answer question 1 about the gist of the article.

This is the first time students have seen the word *paraphrase* as part of the reading comprehension questions. Elicit what paraphrasing is—using different words to say the same thing. If helpful, review the strategies that we use to paraphrase (use of synonyms for key words, use of other words in the same word family, changing the structure of the sentence). To help students with question 7, have them identify the key words or phrases in the sentence and elicit substitutions for each. This will let them see that *c* is the correct answer.

Critical Thinking

Analyzing: Write *Developed Countries* and *Developing Countries* on the board. Elicit characteristics of each from the class and write them under the correct headings. Or, have students do this in pairs. This will help them focus on the topic for analysis. Students should note pollution, availability of cleaning/sanitizing supplies, processed foods, and greater availability of antibiotics as factors contributing to the rise in allergies. In developing countries, there is more exposure to microbes/bacteria, less processed food, and sometimes fewer environmental pollutants.

Discussion: Rhetorical questions can be found throughout a text and are often used to introduce a new topic and to engage the reader. When rhetorical questions come at the end of a text, they function in the way most effective conclusions do—to broaden the topic, suggesting implications, and encouraging prediction.

Reading Skill

Completion: Before students complete the task in the book, go over the information in the box with books closed. Write *Causes of Allergies* in a circle on the board and draw several lines radiating from the circle. Elicit the possible causes and write them on the board. Then have students open the book and check their ideas against the concept map on page 69.

Challenge: For students who have completed the comprehension and reading skill activities, suggest they create a concept map for the passage "Mending Broken Hearts." Additional challenge activities are available on the course website.

Vocabulary Practice

A. Completion: Students complete a reading passage by choosing words from the box. Have students use their knowledge of word endings to identify the parts of speech of the words in the box. For example, *-ent, -tion* are often endings for nouns; *-able, -al* for adjectives; and *-ate* for verbs. The words are in the same form as in the passage and do not need to be changed to a different part of speech, although verbs will change for tense or subject agreement.

B. Definitions: *Register* has a different meaning in question 4 and in the passage than the one students are probably most used to. Direct students to line 90 to guess the meaning from context. In question 3, students have to use the passive voice and so, the past participial form of *suppress.*

Thesaurus
This is the first time students have seen a *Thesaurus* box. Elicit how a thesaurus is different from a regular dictionary, and when it might be useful. Point out that it is especially helpful in writing and other situations where paraphrasing is important. Have students write sentences for each of the words and share them in pairs.

VIEWING: Fighting Malaria

Video Summary: One of the world's most dangerous diseases is malaria, which kills one to two million children per year and affects millions of other people. One surprising new weapon in the war on malaria is a type of chrysanthemum that can kill mosquitoes, the carriers of the disease.

Answer Key

Before You Watch
A. Answers will vary for all items.
B. Answers may vary. Possibilities include: Malaria is a disease. Its symptoms include fever, chills, and flu-like illness. It is caused by a parasite carried by a mosquito. Malaria is very common in most parts of Africa and in some parts of Asia, South America, and Central America.
C. Answers will vary.

While You Watch
A. 5, 3, 1, 6, 2, 4
B. 1. b; **2.** b; **3.** c; **4.** b; **5.** c

After You Watch
1. Answers will vary. Possibilities include: When dried, it kills the mosquito that carries the illness. **2.** Answers will vary. Possibilities include: Farmers earn money. They can then spend more on other things. The shippers also make money.

Teaching Notes

Before You Watch
For suggestions on building students' viewing skills, see page 16.

Flowers may differ around the world, and various cultures will use different flowers for different purposes. In part A, use the photos to review the names of flowers with the class. When students finish their discussion, call on students to share their ideas with the class as to what flower is used for which purpose.

Part C may be difficult for students to answer as it is unlikely they know about the pyrethrum. Have them focus on the causes and/or symptoms of malaria as they make their predictions.

While You Watch
Follow these steps:

1. Students watch the video through once, and complete the sequencing activity.
2. Before playing the video a second time, ask students to try to answer the While You Watch questions in part B.
3. After they've watched the video a second time, students check answers with a partner.
4. If necessary, play the video through a third time. Then check answers as a class.

After You Watch
Students discuss the questions in pairs. Call on students to share their ideas with the class.

Unit 4

Vanishing Cities

Unit Introduction

This unit focuses on the dangers faced by coastal cities. Students first read about the low-lying city of Venice and the threat posed by tourists. Then students learn about the threat that coastal areas face from rising sea levels due to climate change.

Key Words for Internet Research:
Venice, Piazza San Marco, tourism in Venice, climate change, rising seas, Hurricane Sandy, Delta Works

For More Information:
http://ngm.nationalgeographic.com/2009/08/venice/newman-text
http://ngm-beta.nationalgeographic.com/archive/rising-seas-how-they-are-changing-our-coastlines/

Warm Up

Answer Key

1. Answers will vary. **2.** Answers will vary. Possibilities include: coastal cities, New York, Miami, Venice, the Netherlands, India, Vietnam. **3.** Answers will vary. Possibilities include: the Philippines, New York, New Orleans, China, Argentina, Brazil, Mumbai, Kolkata, Jakarta, Guangzhou, Ho Chi Minh City.

Teaching Notes

Before students discuss the Warm Up questions, have the class look at the photo and read the caption. Ask them:

- **Where is the Statue of Liberty?** In New York Harbor.
- **What is the Statue of Liberty?** The Statue of Liberty was a gift from France to the United States. The figure is a robed female representing Libertas, the Roman goddess of freedom.
- **How tall is it?** 305 feet, or 93 meters.
- **Does the picture accurately reflect the information in the caption?** Not exactly—the water would probably be higher on the statue if it rose by 200 feet.
- **Why use the Statue of Liberty to introduce the topic?** It is a recognizable landmark, and because it is tall, it is easy to show rising water.
- **What other images could show the impact of rising sea levels?** Answers will vary. Possibilities include: a map of land underwater, another famous landmark by the sea such as Piazza San Marco, the Sydney Opera House, London Bridge.

Put students in pairs or small groups to discuss the Warm Up questions. Finally, elicit some answers from the class.

Lesson 4A City Under Siege

Lesson Overview

Target Vocabulary: complement, elevated, framed, implement, impose, inadequate, inflict, maximize, sentimental, so-called

Reading Passage Summary: The passage covers the threat to Venice posed by the increasing number of tourists who come to see the picturesque city of canals. Tourism is driving out the residents who can no longer afford to live in a city that caters to wealthy travelers. The costs of maintaining the beauty of a city that is subject to flooding are high, making it very expensive to live in Venice. In addition, services for tourists drive out local businesses.

Answer Key

Before You Read

A. 1. c; **2.** c; **3.** a

B. b

Reading Comprehension

1. c; **2.** c; **3.** a (lines 16–20); **4.** b (line 47); **5.** b (lines 63–67); **6.** a; **7.** a

Reading Skill

1. L; **2.** F; **3.** F; **4.** L; **5.** L; **6.** F; **7.** F; **8.** F; **9.** L; **10.** L; **11.** F; **12.** F

Vocabulary Practice

A. 1. framed; **2.** sentimental; **3.** inflicts; **4.** maximize; **5.** elevated; **6.** impose; **7.** implemented; **8.** inadequate; **9.** so-called

B. 1. inflict; **2.** maximize; **3.** inadequate; **4.** framed; **5.** sentimental; **6.** complement; **7.** elevated; **8.** implement; **9.** so-called; **10.** impose

Teaching Notes

Before You Read

Have students look at the photo before they read the information. Ask them where it is [Venice], and how they know [the gondolas]. To help students connect to the topic, ask students if they have ever been to Venice. Activate background knowledge by eliciting what they already know about Venice, focusing on what makes it attractive to tourists.

A. Quiz: Put students in small groups and have them discuss the quiz questions. It is unlikely students will know the answers, so encourage them to make informed guesses.

B. Skimming: Review how to skim. If students look at the first sentence of every paragraph, they will notice that *tourist* and *tourism* appear often.

Reading Comprehension

Multiple Choice: Question 1 focuses on the main idea and in essence has students confirm their answer in B of Before You Read. In question 2, three of the answers have correct information. However, *a* and *b* only convey half of the relevant information, which makes *c* the best answer. Question 3 asks students to make an inference, so they are working with information that is not stated directly. Answers *b–d* may be true, but there is no evidence in the passage to support them. Answer *a* is supported by facts provided in the passage (80,000 tourists vs. 60,000 residents).

Critical Thinking

Evaluating: This question asks for students' opinions. It might be helpful for them to go through the passage and note specific evidence that supports the main idea. Elicit what constitutes good evidence (statistics, facts) vs. opinion.

Analyzing: This is a two-part question. In the first part, students could complete a T-chart with the author's ideas. When students answer the second part, they can add to the chart.

Reading Skill

A. Classification: Figurative language suggests a comparison between two things. Sometimes the comparison is direct, as with similes that use *as* or *like* (e.g., *I'm as hungry as a bear, he runs like a racehorse*). Indirect comparisons often use verbs in an unusual way to suggest what is being compared.

In the example in the book, the use of *plow* compares the movement of a ship with a plow.

B. Applying: If students find this difficult, encourage them first to write a literal sentence describing their city or region. Then have them change the sentence to include figurative language.

Vocabulary Practice
A. Completion: Students can use their knowledge of word parts to help them with these exercises. In many cases, *im-* or *in-* means "not" as in *impossible* or *inadequate.* In *implement* and *impose,* it means "in" or "on" (to fill in/up, or complete, to put in). The meaning of *in-* in *inflict* is similar (to strike on or against). *Implement* and *complement* also have overlapping meaning coming from the Latin ("to fill up" and "that which fills up").

B. Definitions: *Impose* and *inflict* are very similar in meaning. *Inflict* carries the added meaning of something unwelcome or unbearable.

Usage
These words are frequently confused by students and even by native speakers. *Compliment* is a speech act and so will always have a person subject. *Complement* can be used with a great variety of subjects.

Lesson 4B Rising Seas

Lesson Overview

Target Vocabulary: ambitious, barrier, comply, dire, envision, policy, retreat, surge, take for granted, withstand

Reading Passage Summary: In the first passage, students learned about a coastal city threatened by tourism. Here they learn about coastal cities that are endangered by climate change and rising sea levels. In particular, the passage looks at New York in the aftermath of Hurricane Sandy and the Netherlands in the mid-20th century.

Answer Key

Before You Read
A. 1. Answers will vary. Possibilities include: rising sea levels, more severe weather, threats to plants and animals. **2.** Answers will vary. Possibilities include: restrict use of fossil fuels, greater use of alternative sources of energy.
B. Predictions will vary. Actual answers:
1. A storm surge caused by Hurricane Sandy in New York in 2012. **2.** Coastal cities (e.g., New York, London, Rotterdam) face a greater frequency of devastating storms because of climate change and need to be protected or they won't survive. **3.** A devastating storm in 1953 forced the Netherlands to take drastic action to protect their coasts, including the Delta Works (dikes and barriers) and Rotterdam's Floating Pavilion (a model of floating architecture).
4. Even if we take steps to protect these cities, rising seas may force people to move away from endangered coastline.

Reading Comprehension
1. a; **2.** d (lines 6–9); **3.** d; **4.** a (page 86); **5.** b (lines 132–135); **6.** b (page 88); **7.** c

Reading Skill
B. 1. The author thinks the issue is very important; dramatically, drastically, fleeing; **2.** The other doesn't provide exact figures for numbers and dates, so we don't know how accurate it is. Also, no source is given. **3.** Hal Wanless is chair of the University of Miami's Department of Geological Science, and Klaus Jacob is a Columbia University geophysicist, so they are both good sources of information. **4.** Answers will vary.

Vocabulary Practice
A. 1. envision; **2.** dire; **3.** policy; **4.** take for granted; **5.** withstand; **6.** retreat; **7.** ambitious; **8.** barriers; **9.** surges
B. 1. comply; **2.** retreat; **3.** surge; **4.** policy; **5.** withstand; **6.** ambitious; **7.** envision

Teaching Notes

Before You Read

Have students look at the photo. Elicit other things that are frequently damaged in floods.

A. Discussion: To make sure students understand terms and the issue, review what global warming is and why it is occurring. When you go over the answers, write students' ideas about laws on the board.

B. Skimming and Predicting: Give students a time limit of 1 or 2 minutes for this exercise, to ensure they skim the passage rather than read in detail. When students write in their own words, it is a chance to practice paraphrasing, which they learned about in an earlier unit. After completing the exercise, have students read through the whole article carefully to check their predictions.

Reading Comprehension

Have students answer the comprehension questions individually. Check answers as a class, asking students to give evidence for their answers using line numbers from the reading passage.

For question 3, remind students of the definition of *figurative language* as encountered in Lesson A, Reading Skill. Sentence *a* includes the word *maul*, used figuratively, and sentences *b* and *c* both contain similes: "like another planet" in *b*, and "becoming a kind of Venice" in *c*. Sentence *d* is therefore the correct option, with the word *retreat* used with its literal meaning, "to move away."

Critical Thinking

Analyzing: The second question elaborates on the first. Students need to discuss why they think he says Isaac was a victory. Students should understand that he doesn't mean the storm was a victory, but rather the results of the storm, or the lack of destruction. Specifically, it was a victory for the levee system.

Discussion: For students to discuss this question, you may need to spend some time with the map. Focus on the way the projected map differs from the actual map today. You may need to display a current map, or direct students to one online. They will be much better able to discuss the implications of global warming if they can compare the two situations.

Reading Skill

A. Reading Critically: Go over the information in the box and elicit the ways in which students have already been reading critically. They should notice that all of the critical thinking tasks help them do this. Focus on the new information in the box, which students should read twice, each time with a different purpose.

B. Discussion: After students have read the excerpt in part A, have them discuss the questions in B in pairs. The questions are designed to encourage critical thinking, prompting students to identify persuasive language (*dramatically*, *drastically*, *fleeing*) and to scrutinize the author's use of evidence.

Vocabulary Practice

A. Completion: Students complete a reading passage by choosing words from the box. Students can refer to the passage to guess meaning from context. The target word *envision* has an ending that might suggest it is a noun, but it is a verb.

Retreat can be both a noun and verb. Ask students how it functions in the passage and in the exercise.

B. Definitions: In exercise B, students simply refer to A or the passage to determine meaning and assign words to definitions.

Word Link

Have students write sentences using each of the words. Ask for volunteers to write sentences on the board.

VIEWING: Time and Tide

Video Summary: Smith Island, in the Chesapeake Bay, is threatened by global warming and rising sea waters. Many of the islanders are fishermen whose living depends on catching crabs, and the populations of both are decreasing. Over the next century, very little may be left of the island(s).

Answer Key

Before You Watch

A. 1. a; **2.** b; **3.** a; **4.** a

B. 1. Answers may vary. Possibilities include: fishermen, people who catch crabs.; **2.** Answers may vary. Possibilities include: loss of land, loss of jobs, floods.

While You Watch

A. Smith Island is vulnerable to the ocean. Its land is being eroded, and this is difficult for its inhabitants. Rising seas may one day make the island unfit to live on.

B. 1. 500; **2.** one foot; **3.** century; **4.** building barriers to slow erosion; **5.** there will only be a few high spots left

After You Watch

1.–3. Answers will vary. Crab catches could be small due to increased water temperatures as a result of global warming, which may disrupt the crabs' habitat and ecosystem. It's possible the rising sea level would have a similar effect.

Teaching Notes

Before You Watch

For suggestions on building students' viewing skills, see page 16.

A. Students use context to guess the meaning of new words. Allow them to work individually before checking answers as a class.

B. Have students read the paragraph in activity A once more if necessary and look at the picture. Students should surmise that islanders are probably fishermen. The topics encountered in the two reading passages of this unit should enable them to answer question 2.

While You Watch

Follow these steps:

1. Allow students some time to read the options in part A before watching the video through once, and checking the main idea.
2. Before playing the video a second time, ask students to try to answer the While You Watch questions in part B.
3. After they've watched the video a second time, students check answers with a partner.
4. If necessary, play the video through a third time. Then check answers as a class.

After You Watch

Students discuss the questions in pairs. Call on students to share their ideas with the class.

Unit 5

Eco-Living

Unit Introduction

This unit focuses on how we can live in more eco-friendly ways, primarily by reducing our usage of fossil fuels. Students first learn about a couple who spent a month trying to reduce their own personal carbon footprint. Then students read about projects using solar energy.

Key Words for Internet Research: *carbon footprint, CO_2 emissions, Nevada Solar One, solar energy, National Renewable Energy Laboratory, photovoltaic panels, Solarseidlung, solar energy in Germany*

For More Information:
http://ngm-beta.nationalgeographic.com/archive/saving-energy-it-starts-at-home
http://ngm-beta.nationalgeographic.com/archive/plugging-into-the-sun

Warm Up

Answer Key

1. Answers will vary. Possibilities include: oil, coal, natural gas, nuclear, solar, wind.
2. Answers will vary. Possibilities include:
Fossil fuels (oil, coal, gas): Advantages: Available technology; Disadvantages: Impact on environment, limited supplies
Nuclear: Advantages: Potential large supply; Disadvantages: Expensive technology, safety
Solar: Advantages: Clean and sustainable; Disadvantages: Current technology is inefficient; it's not always sunny
Wind: Advantages: Clean and sustainable; Disadvantages: Some think turbines are unsightly; not everywhere in the world has strong enough winds
3. Answers will vary. Possibilities include: drive less, walk and cycle more, recycle waste, buy local.

Teaching Notes

Before students discuss the Warm Up questions, have the class look at the photo and read the caption. Ask them:

- **What does urban agriculture mean?** Growing food in cities.
- **Where can people grow food/have gardens in cities?** In some cities, people have rooftop gardens. This cuts down on heating and cooling costs for the building while also providing food. Many cities have urban gardens in vacant lots or parts of public parks.
- **What are the advantages and disadvantages of urban agriculture?** In addition to reducing transportation costs, advantages include low-cost and organic food, activity/exercise, community building. Disadvantages might include: small scale, limited growing season.

Finally, put students in pairs or small groups to discuss the Warm Up questions.

Lesson 5A Carbon Footprint

Lesson Overview

Target Vocabulary: appliance, audit, commonplace, commute, compact, mode, obstacle, pioneer, threshold, utility

Reading Passage Summary: The passage describes an experiment conducted by Peter Miller and his wife. They spent a month trying to reduce their carbon footprint. First, they analyzed what their footprint probably was and looked at the ways in which their home might be energy-inefficient. Then they used strategies to lower their energy usage.

Answer Key

Before You Read

A. 1. T; **2.** T; **3.** F (Kuwait); **4.** F (Estonia)
B. 1. Tracking and reducing carbon dioxide output; **2.** They could cut their output.

Reading Comprehension

1. b; **2.** c; **3.** b (lines 12–15); **4.** d (lines 24–28)
5. d (lines 85–88); **6.** a; **7.** d

Reading Skill

A. 1. f; **2.** c; **3.** d; **4.** b
B. 1. a; **2.** g; **3.** e; **4.** h

Vocabulary Practice

A. 1. threshold; **2.** commonplace; **3.** pioneered; **4.** audit; **5.** obstacles
B. 1. utility; **2.** commonplace; **3.** appliances; **4.** mode; **5.** obstacles; **6.** compact, commute

Teaching Notes

Before You Read

Have students look at the photo before they read the information. Ask students if they think New York City is typical of most cities. Have students support their answers with reasons.

A. True or False: Students need to understand the graphic to answer these questions. Have students check their answers in pairs to confirm their understanding before you go over the answers with the class.

B. Skimming and Predicting: The caption will tell students most of what they need to answer the questions, but they should skim the whole article to confirm.

Reading Comprehension

Multiple Choice: Have students read the entire passage silently and answer the comprehension questions. Check answers as a class, asking students to give evidence for their answers using line numbers from the reading passage.

Question 1 focuses on the gist and will confirm students' predictions in part B of Before You Read. When students answer question 4, the correct answer hinges on the word *initially*. The author's initial response to the idea of reducing his family's CO_2 production by 80% is that "it seemed unlikely to me, too," which reflects answer *d*. He later agrees to the 80% reduction, reflecting answer *a*; however, this is not his *initial* reaction and is therefore incorrect.

In question 6, students work with paraphrasing. Review the strategies for paraphrasing (use of synonyms, different word forms, etc.). Have students identify key words in the sentence and look for synonyms (e.g., *trimmed – reduced*). They will need to understand the relationship between twice as much of A and half as much of B.

Critical Thinking

Analyzing: Students need to recognize the author's attitude and provide support for their answers. Authors frequently reveal attitudes in their conclusions. Paragraphs L, M, N, and R suggest that he is fairly positive.

Discussion: This asks students to relate the topic to their own lives. Elicit specific examples of where they use a lot of energy and why it would be difficult to reduce that usage.

Reading Skill

A. and B. Matching: Make sure students understand that a thesis identifies the topic, but also includes a controlling idea. Students typically have greater difficulty with controlling ideas than with topics. In part A, students choose four sentences from the list as main ideas for each section. The other four sentences will be used in part B as supporting information. Suggest students read all eight sentences and note which are more general and which more specific before they do either exercise.

Challenge: For students who have completed the reading comprehension and skill activities, have them add other details to the supporting information for each main idea.

Vocabulary Practice

A. Completion: Both *audit* and *pioneer* can be used as either a noun or verb. Have students read through the text to identify the part of speech needed in each case. *Commonplace* is a compound word formed from the adjective *common* and the noun *place.* It is also an adjective, although students may misidentify it as a noun.

B. Completion: *Utility* is a noun, but used as an adjective/noun modifier in question 1.

Word Partnership

Have students work in pairs to use the word partners in the box in sentences. Call on students to share sentences with the class.

Lesson 5B Plugging into the Sun

Lesson Overview

Target Vocabulary: circulate, deadline, ingenious, manufacture, offset, panel, premium, renewable, subtract, yield

Reading Passage Summary: This passage covers advances being made in the use of solar energy. It focuses on two locations: the U.S., specifically Nevada Solar One outside of Las Vegas, and Germany where the government pays residents to produce solar energy.

Answer Key

Before You Read

A. 1. China, U.S., Germany, Spain, India; **2.** Germany; **3.** China; **4.** Answers will vary.
B. 1. the United States and Germany; **2.** Nevada Solar One and its 182,000 mirrors, and Freiburg's Solarsiedlung, a "solar settlement"

Reading Comprehension

1. c (lines 7–8); **2.** d (lines 31–33); **3.** b; **4.** c; **5.** c; **6.** cq **7.** a

Reading Skill

a. G (paragraph L); **b.** G (lines 28–29); **c.** N; **d.** U (lines 55–58); **e.** N; **f.** U (lines 100–103); **g.** G (lines 151–160); **h.** G (paragraph M); **i.** U (lines 155–157); **j.** B (paragraphs P and G); **k.** U (lines 161–164); **l.** U (lines 169–176)

Vocabulary Practice

A. 1. ingenious; **2.** renewable; **3.** yield; **4.** circulation; **5.** premium
B. 1. manufacture; **2.** deadline; **3.** subtract; **4.** premium; **5.** panel; **6.** offset; **7.** circulate

Teaching Notes

Before You Read

A. Understanding Maps: After you go over the answers, have students work in pairs to take turns asking and answering other questions about the map.

B. Scan: After students identify the kinds of sites mentioned in the article, elicit what that information suggests about approaches to solar power (i.e., a huge area with hundreds of thousands of mirrors vs. a "solar settlement" of individual homes with solar panels.)

Reading Comprehension

Multiple Choice: Have students read the entire passage silently and answer the comprehension questions. Check answers as a class, asking students to give evidence for their answers using line numbers from the reading passage. Ask students to explain the strategies they used in answering the questions.

In making inferences with vocabulary, such as in question 3, students should use context as well as dictionaries as needed. In this case, *barely tapped* means that only a small part of a much larger supply has been used.

Remind students that in answering questions with *NOT,* they are basically confirming that three answers are correct. All four answers in 4 are mentioned in the paragraph, but government subsidies should be reduced, not used as a means of cutting prices.

Critical Thinking

Analyzing: As in 5A, students are asked to gauge the author's attitude toward the topic. Review the strategies they used the last time to identify attitude.

Discussion: If necessary, elicit factors influencing a region's suitability for solar power production before students answer the first question.

Reading Skill

Classification: To complete the exercise correctly, students have to search for evidence for each sentence in **both** sections (on the United States and on Germany). Just because it is true for one country does not make it untrue for the other. Students can complete the activity individually. Alternatively, put students in pairs and have one focus on the U.S., and the other on Germany. Then have the students work together to share information about their respective countries and complete the exercise in full.

Challenge: For students who have completed the comprehension and reading skill activities, suggest they create a Venn diagram to compare solar energy in the U.S. and in Germany. They can add the details from the exercise as well as other evidence in the passage.

Vocabulary Practice

A. Completion: Students complete a reading passage by choosing words from the box. The words in the box are used in much the same way as they are in the passage. Students can refer to the passage to guess meaning from context. In the passage, *circulate* and *subtract* are in verb form. In this exercise, students will use the noun forms (*circulation* and *subtraction*).

B. Definitions: In exercise B, students refer to A or the passage to determine meaning and assign words to definitions.

Word Partnership

Elicit examples of premium brands, products, and services.

VIEWING: Eco-Detectives

Video Summary: Amory Lovins and a team of eco-detectives look for ways to save energy in people's homes. He points out inefficiencies and appliances with vampire loads. Lovins is a role model, using solar energy and very little electricity.

Answer Key

Before You Watch

A. 1. c; **2.** g; **3.** f; **4.** d; **5.** b; **6.** e; **7.** a

B. Answers may vary. Possibilities include: unplug appliances/electronics, get energy efficient lightbulbs, insulate the house.

While You Watch

A. The following should be checked: a, d

B. 1. c; **2.** a; **3.** c; **4.** b; **5.** b

After You Watch

1. Answers will vary. **2.** Answers will vary. Possibilities include: Use eco-friendly lightbulbs, unplug appliances, seal doors and windows, use solar panels.

3. Amory Lovins probably means that by taking measures to combat climate change, we can also save money.

Teaching Notes

Before You Watch

For suggestions on building students' viewing skills, see page 16.

A. Students use context to guess the meaning of new words. Check answers as a class.

B. Students can recycle the information they have learned in the unit as well as add their own ideas. Either have students brainstorm with a partner or ask the class as a whole and write their ideas on the board.

While You Watch

Follow these steps:

1. Give students time to read the sentences in part A before playing the video. Then students watch the video through once and check the statements. Note that the answers are not stated directly so must be inferred from information learned in the video.
2. Before playing the video a second time, ask students to try to answer the While You Watch questions in part B.
3. After they've watched the video a second time, students check answers with a partner.
4. If necessary, play the video through a third time. Then check answers as a class.

After You Watch

Have students discuss the questions in pairs or small groups. Call on students to share their ideas with the class.

Unit 6 Wildlife in Trouble

Unit Introduction

This unit focuses on endangered wildlife. In Lesson A, students learn about one particular species, the bluefin tuna, and what scientists are learning about it. Then they read about endangered species in general and think about how we decide which species to help.

Key Words for Internet Research: *bluefin tuna, Tuna Research and Conservation Center, tagging, Bronx Zoo, Cincinnati Zoo, San Diego Zoo, the Frozen Zoo*

For More Information:
http://channel.nationalgeographic.com/channel/wicked-tuna/articles/bluefin-tuna-101/
http://ngm-beta.nationalgeographic.com/2014/03/articles/quicksilver/

Warm Up

Answer Key

1. Answers will vary. Possibilities include: tiger, several kinds of rhino, mountain gorilla, orangutan; disappearing habitats and poaching. **2.** Answers will vary. **3.** Answers will vary. Possibilities include: koala, grizzly bear, condor, bald eagle, bison.

Teaching Notes

Before students discuss the Warm Up questions, have the class look at the photo and read the caption. Ask them:

- **Where are the Galapagos Islands?** Off the coast of Chile and Ecuador.
- **What is special about them?** Because they are relatively far from mainland, the islands are home to some unique animals. Many tourists go to see the wildlife. Charles Darwin visited the Galapagos Islands in the 19th century and based his ideas about evolution in part on what he saw there.
- **What do you know about tortoises?** Tortoises are land-dwelling turtles. They have the longest known lifespan of any animal—up to 150 years. Most Pinta Island tortoises were killed by hunters in the 19th century. Although Lonesome George was the last known Pinta Island tortoise, 17 first-generation hybrids have been found, giving researchers hope that some of their purebred parents are still alive.

Put students in pairs or small groups to discuss the Warm Up questions. Have the class brainstorm a list of endangered animals and write their ideas on the board.

Lesson 6A Quicksilver

Lesson Overview

Target Vocabulary: collaboration, deserted, detrimental, gear, haul, mingling, scholar, shield, startling, turbulence

Reading Passage Summary: The passage discusses the plight of the bluefin tuna, a huge fish that is hunted, usually for sushi, and sold for thousands of dollars per fish. Researchers tag the fish to learn more about their movements. Wise management is needed to protect the species.

Answer Key

Before You Read

A. 1. Answers will vary; **2.** Answers will vary. Possibilities include: overfishing, different regulations in various countries, toxicity of fish both wild-caught and farmed; **3.** Answers will vary. Possibilities include: regulation/bans, farming, protection of habitats

B. Answers will vary. Possibilities include: **1.** Bluefin tuna are large and powerful; **2.** People catch and tag the huge fish; **3.** Where bluefin tuna move around the world; **4.** The possibility that the tuna will become extinct

Reading Comprehension

1. c; **2.** d; **3.** b; **4.** a; **5.** d (lines 111–113); **6.** a (lines 132–137); **7.** a

Reading Skill

1. a; **2.** a; **3.** a; **4.** b; **5.** a; **6.** a; **7.** b; **8.** b; **9.** a; **10.** b; **11.** b; **12.** a; **13.** b; **14.** b; **15.** a

Vocabulary Practice

A. 1. startling; **2.** hauled; **3.** gear; **4.** collaborate; **5.** scholar; **6.** detrimental

B. 1. a; **2.** b; **3.** a; **4.** b; **5.** b

Teaching Notes

Before You Read

Have students look at the photo before they read the information. Ask students why they think bluefin tuna are being overfished. Have them read the caption/information below. Ask: *What are the advantages or disadvantages of the practice described?*

A: **Discussion:** After students discuss the questions in pairs, call on students to share their ideas with the class.

B. Skim and Predict: To help students with paraphrasing and/or identifying topics, have them write alternate titles for each section.

Reading Comprehension

Multiple Choice: Have students read the entire passage silently and answer the comprehension questions. Check answers as a class, asking students to give evidence for their answers using line numbers from the reading passage.

Sometimes questions about figurative language can be tricky, as in 1. Here the use of *drive* in c is not figurative language, but a common use of the verb (to propel forcefully). However, it might confuse students because we usually think of the other meaning (to drive a car) and this might sound figurative. Note that question 6 refers specifically to *western* bluefin tuna, which cannot be found in the Mediterranean. Only *eastern* bluefin tuna are found there.

Point out that place can function to organize ideas. In the concluding section (addressed in question 7), the writer associates the location of Hopkins Marine Station with the abandoned canneries nearby. This physical association provides a way for the writer to compare the fates of the two species, and suggest implications.

Critical Thinking

Evaluating: Direct students to paragraph C as needed. Extend the task by asking students to give examples of other animals with an ancient history of interaction with humans.

Discussion: The questions focus on feelings, rather than facts, but students should still support their opinions with evidence from the passage or from other knowledge they have.

Reading Skill

Definitions: Elicit some examples of homonyms from the class to introduce the activity. Ensure that students refer back to the article and use context to help them choose the correct answers.

Vocabulary Practice

A. Completion: Suggest students find the words in the passage to guess their meaning from context. Most of the words in the exercise are used with much the same meaning and form. *Mingling* is a gerund in the passage, and here is presented as an adjective in 1 and a verb in 4.

B. Words in Context: *Shield* can be both a noun and a verb that have similar meanings.

Word Link

Have students work in pairs to use the words in the box in sentences. Call on students to share sentences with the class.

Lesson 6B Building the Ark

Lesson Overview

Target Vocabulary: captive, extinction, imminent, oblivion, refuge, shrink, state-of-the-art, struggle, supplement, tide

Reading Passage Summary: This passage covers the efforts zoos are making to preserve animals in danger of becoming extinct. Most of these efforts focus on breeding programs, such as the one at the Bronx Zoo that helped save the bison. In some cases, the programs reintroduce the species to the wild. Another effort involves freezing genetic material in case living animals of the species do become extinct.

Answer Key

Before You Read

A. 1. Answers will vary. Possibilities include: captive breeding; **2.** Answers will vary. Possibilities include: popularity, size, familiarity
B. 1. Cincinnati Zoo; **2.** Bronx Zoo; **3.** Miller Park Zoo; **4.** Bronx Zoo, Toledo Zoo; **5.** San Diego Zoo/Frozen Zoo; **6.** San Diego Zoo

Reading Comprehension

1. c; **2.** d (lines 67–70); **3.** b; **4.** a (lines 101–108; **5.** d; **6.** c (lines 150–157); **7.** b (lines 172–175)

Reading Skill

A. 1. a; **2.** b; **3.** b; **4.** a; **5.** c
B. Greek Root: **1.** self; **2.** earth; **3.** write; **4.** study of; **5.** sound; **6.** see; **7.** distant
Latin Root: **1.** sound/hear; **2.** speak; **3.** carry; **4.** feel; **5.** write; **6.** earth; **7.** see

Vocabulary Practice

A. 1. extinct; **2.** shrinking; **3.** struggling; **4.** Imminent; **5.** refuge; **6.** oblivion; **7.** captive;
B. 1. imminent; **2.** supplement; **3.** captive; **4.** state-of-the-art; **5.** refuge; **6.** Oblivion; **7.** tide

Teaching Notes

Before You Read

A. Discussion: To draw on students' experiences, ask them what animals they like to see at zoos and why. Elicit the animals that they think are most popular at zoos.

B. Scan: Have students identify the paragraph or line where they found the information.

Reading Comprehension

Multiple Choice: Have students read the entire passage silently and answer the comprehension questions. Check answers as a class, asking students to give evidence for their answers using line numbers from the reading passage.

The first question may be difficult for some students because the passage touches on three out of four of the questions *(a, b, c)* to some degree. However, students should see that the subtitle *Who to Save?* makes the answer clear. For added challenge, have students discuss all the ethical questions in small groups.

Question 4 is the first time students have seen a cause and effect question. Elicit what word in the question helps them identify it as a cause and effect question (*prompt*). Elicit other words that make this relationship clear (e.g., *cause, effect, factor, results in, influences, affects*).

To help with question 5, have students look at the sentence and identify what it is doing (giving specific statistics about species that are endangered). Ask: *What should the sentence before this do?* (Give a more general statement about the danger species face).

Critical Thinking

Evaluating: This asks students to judge the relative success of the Kihansi spray toad program. Students should think about their criteria for evaluating as they share their ideas.

Discussion: This gets at a fundamental question: Why should we save animals?

Reading Skill

A. Identifying: Students have already worked with this skill in previous units through the boxes for Word Links, Thesaurus, etc. Have students match the word root to the correct meaning. When checking answers, elicit other words with the same word roots. Examples may include: 1. nutrients, nutritious; 2. biology, biography; 3. kilometer, millimeter; 4. zoology, zoonotic; 5. hydroponics, hydrotherapy.

Completion: Have students complete the chart with a partner. Students may benefit from using a dictionary to check the meaning of unknown words.

Challenge: For students who have completed the comprehension and reading skill activities, suggest they write their response to one of the questions in Reading Comprehension, item 1. Additional challenge activities are available on the course website.

Vocabulary Practice

A. Completion: Students complete a reading passage by choosing words from the box. Some words have the same form in different parts of speech (*captive, tide, supplement, struggle*). Suggest students read the sentences and identify which part of speech is needed. In item 6, *oblivion* is the correct answer although students could also possibly use the noun form of *extinct* (*extinction*) to complete the sentence.

B. Definitions: In exercise B, students complete definitions. They will not need to change form.

Word Partnership

Have students look up the words and distinguish between shades of meaning. Which one would they use to describe an exam they are nervous about? A book soon to be published, a divorce, a storm?

VIEWING: Life on Ice

Video Summary: Scientists at the Smithsonian preserve specimens in liquid nitrogen to add to their collections. Freezing allows researchers to study the genomes of animals, which can solve questions they have been unable to answer as well as for future research purposes. For example, spiders interest scientists because of their silk and their poisons.

Answer Key

Before You Watch

A. **1.** e; **2.** d; **3.** h; **4.** f; **5.** a; **6.** c; **7.** b; **8.** g
B. Answers may vary. Possibilities include:
1. To study their genomes/genetic information, to preserve the animal's DNA (for cloning, research); **2.** On ice, by freezing them

While You Watch

A. **1.** F; **2.** T; **3.** F; **4.** T; **5.** T
B. **1.** scientific; **2.** frozen; **3.** sequencing; **4.** information; **5.** collection; **6.** liquid; **7.** centralize; **8.** request; **9.** piece

After You Watch

Answers will vary. Possibilities include:
1. Researchers can learn about neurobiology, and they can learn how poisons work in humans. **2.** Someone could misuse the knowledge to create biological weapons. There are also ethical issues associated with the possibility of preserving the DNA for cloning purposes.

Teaching Notes

Before You Watch

For suggestions on building students' viewing skills, see page 16.

A. Students work individually to match the words to their definitions. If necessary, have students consult a dictionary.

B. Give students a short time to read through the information. Then have students discuss the questions with a partner or in small groups. Students can recycle the information they have learned in the unit as well as add their own ideas.

While You Watch

Follow these steps:

1. Allow students some time to read the statements in part A before starting the video. Students watch the video through once and complete their answers. Check answers as a class, eliciting explanations for the sentences students marked as false.
2. Before playing the video a second time, ask students to first read the quotations and think about possible answers.
3. After they've watched the video a second time, students check answers with a partner.
4. If necessary, play the video through a third time. Then check answers as a class.

After You Watch

Students discuss the questions in pairs or small groups. Call on students to share their ideas with the class.

Unit 7

Human Body

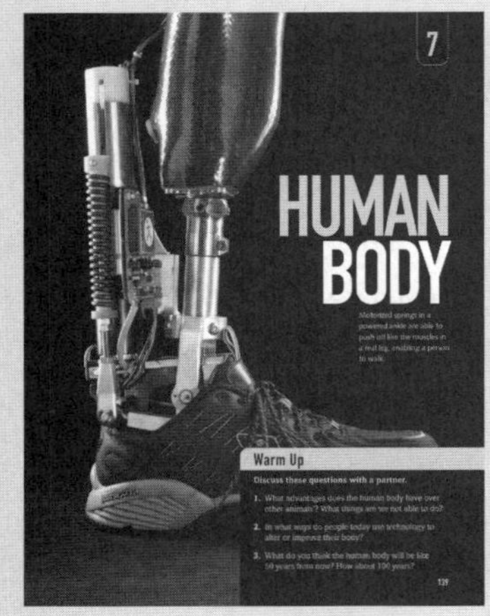

Unit Introduction

This unit focuses on the human body. Students first learn about advances made in mapping the brain. In the second passage, students learn about human bionics through the example of Amanda Kitts, whose bionic arm replaces one lost in an accident.

Key Words for Internet Research:
brain mapping, Van Wedeen, fMRI, Jeff Lichtman, Allen Institute, CLARITY, Rehabilitation Institute of Chicago

For More Information:
http://ngm-beta.nationalgeographic.com/2014/02/articles/secrets-of-the-brain/
http://ngm.nationalgeographic.com/2010/01/bionics/fischman-text

Warm Up

Answer Key

1. Answers will vary. Possibilities include: Humans can walk upright, hold/use tools, they have large brains, but they're not able to fly; **2.** Answers will vary. Possibilities include: Laser surgery to correct vision, cosmetic surgery, joint replacement, pacemakers; **3.** Answers will vary.

Teaching Notes

Before students discuss the Warm Up questions, have the class look at the photo and read the caption. Ask them:

- **What is a spring? How does it work?** Springs are coils, usually of metal, that can compress and when released, exert force outward.
- **Who are some famous people with artificial limbs or prostheses?** Oscar Pistorius is probably the most famous—an Olympic runner from South Africa, who also was tried and convicted of shooting his girlfriend. Other famous athletes include: rock climber Hugh Herr, actress and athlete Aimee Mullins, activist Heather Mills (ex-wife of Paul McCartney).
- **What kind of prosthetic legs/feet do athletes usually use in competition?** For amputations below the knee, many runners use carbon fiber blades. Carbon fiber polymer is very strong and lightweight.

Put students in pairs or small groups to discuss the Warm Up questions. Elicit answers from the class and write the best ideas on the board.

Challenge: As an out-of-class assignment, have students research type of prosthesis or other device that helps individuals compensate for a lost body part. Students prepare a two-minute talk and present in small groups.

Lesson 7A Secrets of the Brain

Lesson Overview

Target Vocabulary: dazzle, disorder, exquisitely, forefront, neural, organ, originate, scrutiny, tricky, unprecedented

Reading Passage Summary: The passage covers research being done on the brain. It discusses imaging using MRI scanning to understand the genetic landscape of human brains. Other researchers have made mouse brains transparent, and then used chemicals to color the neural pathways. Brain mapping has begun to change lives through brain–machine interfaces that allow paralyzed patients to communicate and even "move."

Answer Key

Before You Read

A. 1. Answers will vary. Possibilities include: how it works, which parts of the brain do which things, how individual brains differ from one another, how brains with disorders or injuries work differently; **2.** Answers will vary. Possibilities include: help individuals who are paralyzed, have brain damage, have certain diseases or disorders; could also help prevent some of the diseases or disorders; help identify people with problems; could help society as a whole by helping humans do things they can't do now

B. Answers will vary. Possibilities include: **1.** How the writer participated in brain research/ scanning; **2.** How researchers use technology to look at the brain and see how it works; **3.** How the brain can interact with a machine, paralyzed person using a machine to do things

Reading Comprehension

1. c (lines 17–20); **2.** d; **3.** b (lines 89–90); **4.** a (lines 103–105); **5.** c; **6.** d (lines 134–156); **7.** d (page 146)

Reading Skill

A. is then used, are put in order, is built, is revealed

B. 1. a; **2.** a; **3.** b; **4.** a

Vocabulary Practice

A. 1. organ; **2.** forefront; **3.** neural; **4.** originate; **5.** scrutinize

B. 1. a; **2.** b; **3.** b; **4.** b; **5.** a

Teaching Notes

Before You Read

Have students look at the photo before they read the information. Ask: *How do you think this feels? Would you want to do this? Why or why not?*

A. **Discussion:** Have students look at the photo and read the caption before discussing the questions in pairs or small groups.

B. Skim: Give students one minute to skim the passage and make their predictions.

Reading Comprehension

Multiple Choice: Have students read the entire passage silently and answer the comprehension questions. Check answers as a class, asking students to give evidence for their answers using line numbers from the reading passage.

The question about paraphrasing (2) requires students to make inferences to do this correctly. The clue to understanding Lichtman's meaning in the quote is in the previous sentence which states that the human brain has a thousand times more neurons than a mouse brain.

In question 4, students have to identify the way the author feels about something. Review the kinds of clues students can look for (e.g., the use of subjective adjectives, the use of other sources that hold the same attitude). Two such clues: the first sentence of paragraph J ("perhaps the most remarkable"), and the first sentence of paragraph K ("dazzle," "awestruck").

Critical Thinking

Evaluating: Have students support their ideas with reasons and examples. Make sure students understand that *ramification* is a synonym for *result* or *effect.* If helpful, ask probing questions like *How would people control what doctors/ scientists were doing? What kind of things might people want brain implants to do?*

Discussion: Make sure students understand that a *guinea pig* is someone or something used in research to test things on. Then have them discuss their answers in pairs or small groups.

Reading Skill

A. Noticing: Go over each reason for the passive and ask questions such as: *Who slices the brain? Why doesn't the writer know who left the box of chocolates?* You may want to discuss situations in which the speaker or author wishes to be vague, including when he or she doesn't want to blame someone directly, and when he or she wants to avoid responsibility. Elicit other examples of each use of passive voice.

In completing part A, students need to be able to recognize the passive voice (*be* + past participle). If helpful, review the formation of common tenses.

B. Multiple Choice: In part B, point out that the direction line uses *probably.* It is possible that the writer might have had another purpose. Discuss with students if the other answer is possible and in what situation. For example, in question 1, we might assume the patient's doctor gave him the news. However, other people are possible, such as a nurse, a family member, a surgeon, a social worker.

Challenge: Write the following question on the board for students who have completed the comprehension and reading skill activities. Additional challenge activities are available on the course website.

Would you want to have a brain implant? Why or why not?

Vocabulary Practice

A. Completion: Have students work in pairs to identify word parts they know the meaning of. Three words include *or,* but they do not have the same meaning. In *disorder, ord-* means rank, row, or arrangement. In *originate, or* is part of *origin,* which means beginning. *Organ* is probably derived from the Greek word for work or tool. Elicit which prefixes mean "not" (*dis-* and *un-*). This will help them with part B

B. Words in Context: Have students check their answers by referring back to the passage and substituting their answers in the sentence.

Word Partnership

Have students write a sentence with each of the phrases.

Lesson 7B Human Bionics

Lesson Overview

Target Vocabulary: assigned, crude, embedded, intricate, reasonable, reliable, salvage, sensation, valid, vibrate

Reading Passage Summary: This passage covers the progress being made in the field of human bionics. Amanda lost her arm in a car accident, but now has a bionic arm which she controls with her brain.

Answer Key

Before You Read

A. 1. d; **2.** c; **3.** a; **4.** b

B. Bionic body part: arm

Why she needs it: lost her arm in a car accident

Things she can do now: hold things, pick up big things

Things she can't do yet: pick up small things, have sensations

Reading Comprehension

1. a; **2.** b; **3.** d (lines 49–53); **4.** b (lines 54–55); **5.** b (lines 91–100); **6.** a; **7.** a

Reading Skill

1. F; **2.** O; **3.** F; **4.** F; **5.** O; **6.** O; **7.** F; **8.** O; **9.** O

Vocabulary Practice

A. 1. reliability; **2.** sensation; **3.** intricate; **4.** embedded; **5.** vibrations; **6.** assign; **7.** reasonable

B. 1. a; **2.** b; **3.** b; **4.** a; **5.** b

Teaching Notes

Before You Read

A. Matching: Students need to read the information to complete the task. Some vocabulary may be unfamiliar to students (e.g., artificial, capability, transmit, manipulate, propel, stimulate, capture, convert). Students can use their dictionaries or work in pairs to determine the meaning from context.

B. Skim and Predict: Some students have difficulty skimming for a limited amount of time—they get drawn into reading too much. Tell students you are going to time them for two minutes. Remind students that captions and visuals can help with skimming.

Reading Comprehension

Multiple Choice: Have students read the entire passage silently and answer the comprehension questions. Check answers as a class, asking students to give evidence for their answers using line numbers from the reading passage.

In question 1, elicit why incorrect answers can be ruled out (It's not about robots, it only focuses on one aspect of Amanda Kitt's life, and it doesn't really give the history of prosthetic limbs as it focuses primarily on bionics).

Finding the antecedent for *it* in question 6 may be tricky as this word is used sveral times in the sentence. The first pronoun refers to the process of using her arm as a whole. The next two pronouns refer to the arm rather than the act of moving it.

Critical Thinking

Evaluating: Before students complete the task, ask how they would determine if someone was optimistic or pessimistic. They should note that when optimistic, people point out possibilities and potential. When pessimistic, they focus on problems and barriers.

Discussion: Students can include ideas from previous units and lessons in their discussion as well as other ideas.

Reading Skill

Fact or Opinion: Elicit or provide examples of facts and opinions before students start the activity. When checking answers with the class, highlight the key words that signify opinions, such as the adjective *amazing* in sentence 5. Predictions about the future (sentences 6 and 8) should also be classed as opinions, as the information cannot be verified at the present time.

Challenge: For students who have completed the comprehension and reading skill activities, suggest they look at the passage in 7A and find four examples of facts and four examples of opinions. Additional challenge activities are available on the course website.

Vocabulary Practice

A. Completion: Students complete a reading passage by choosing words from the box. Some of the words will be a different part of speech from their form in the passage (e.g., reliable – reliability, vibrate – vibration, valid – validities, assigned – assign). The other words do not change form. Students can use their knowledge of suffixes to identify parts of speech: *-able* (adjective), *-ability* (noun), - " (noun), *-ity* (noun).

B. Words in Context: In exercise B, students complete definitions. They will not need to change from. *Salvage* comes from the same root as *save*, but it often refers to goods, as in rescuing goods from a wrecked ship. In question 4, the best answer is *a*, because you are saving, or able to use, something from the situation.

Word Link

Ask students to find other words with *val* (e.g., *validate, validity, valuable*).

VIEWING: Bionic Mountaineer

Video Summary: Hugh Herr is an amputee who climbs mountains and designs prosthetics at MIT. As a boy, he went hiking with a friend. They got lost for three days in the snow and ice. Hugh got frostbite, and his legs were amputated below the knee. He didn't give up climbing, however. Instead, he designed legs that would help him climb better. He is now borrowing ideas from the animal world to design better prostheses.

Answer Key

Before You Watch

A. a. 4; **b.** 1; **c.** 3; **d.** 5; **e.** 2

B. Answers may vary. Possibilities include:

1. Falling from height; bad weather; getting lost;

2. Less control, no sensation so hard to feel the rock beneath.

While You Watch

A. 1. a; **2.** b; **3.** c

B. 1. F; **2.** O; **3.** F; **4.** F; **5.** O; **6.** O

After You Watch

1. Answers will vary. **2.** Answers will vary. Possibilities include: unfair advantage in sports or other activities, against religious beliefs, issues of liability/responsibility;

3. Answers will vary.

Teaching Notes

Before You Watch

For suggestions on building students' viewing skills, see page 16.

A. Students match words to definitions getting meaning from context.

B. Students can use their imagination or knowledge of other activities to answer question 2.

While You Watch

Follow these steps:

1. Students watch the video through once and complete part A.
2. Before playing the video a second time, ask students to try to answer the While You Watch questions in part B.
3. After they've watched the video a second time, students check answers with a partner.
4. If necessary, play the video through a third time. Then check answers as a class.

After You Watch

Students discuss the questions in pairs. Call on students to share their ideas with the class. For question 2, ensure that students understand that the term *ethical issues* relates to things that people consider to be right or wrong. For example, some people may believe that it is wrong to alter our bodies due to religious beliefs.

Unit 8 Social Behavior

Unit Introduction

This unit addresses social behavior, specifically in insects. Students read first about the social behavior of both ants and bees and how they are similar to humans. In the second passage, they read an interview with the noted naturalist Edward O. Wilson.

Key Words for Internet Research:
ant colonies, bee colonies, Iain Couzin, Air Liquide, Thomas D. Seeley, Edward O. Wilson, the Superorganism

For More Information:
http://ngm-beta.nationalgeographic.com/archive/the-ant-and-her-world/
http://news.nationalgeographic.com/news/2006/03/0327_060327_eo_wilson.html

Warm Up

Answer Key

1. Answers will vary. Possibilities include: Dating, office politics, religion; **2.** Answers will vary. Possibilities include: Chimpanzees, gorillas, monkeys, elephants, dogs, dolphins; **3.** Answers will vary. Possibilities include: Insects sometimes live in social groups and have different jobs.

Teaching Notes

Before students answer the Warm Up questions, have the class look at the photo and read the caption. Ask them:

- **What kind of animal is a meerkat?** Meerkats are small mammals in the mongoose family. They eat insects and other small animals.
- **Where does it live?** Primarily in southern countries in Africa, including the Kalahari Desert and the Namib Desert.
- **What social behaviors do meerkats have?** They live in groups of about 20 called mobs, clans, or gangs, but the group can be much larger. They live in large networks of tunnels. Meerkats are very social. They groom each other and share different responsibilities. Some stand sentry while others are foraging or playing. Some tutor and babysit the young meerkats.

Put students in groups or pairs to discuss the Warm Up questions. Elicit answers from the class and note any useful vocabulary on the board.

Lesson 8A The Genius of Swarms

Lesson Overview

Target Vocabulary: aggregate, coherent, code, criteria, faculty, imitate, index, protocol, secure, territory

Reading Passage Summary: This passage discusses the social behavior of ants and bees, explaining that individuals are not very intelligent, but the colonies are. This is because the individuals play a role in a larger whole. No single individual is in charge or makes decisions; rather the group works together to perform key functions such as locating food or choosing a new home.

Answer Key

Before You Read

A. 1. a. bees; **b.** elephants; **c.** lions; **d.** fish
2. Answers will vary. Possible advantages include: protection from predators, division of labor, cooperation; Possible disadvantages include: overcrowding, fighting over resources
B. Answers will vary. Possibilities include: ants—transportation and distribution systems; bees—running meetings, making decisions.

Reading Comprehension

1. b; **2.** a; **3.** c; **4.** b (lines 23–24); **5.** c (lines 69–70); **6.** b; **7.** b (lines 34–35 and lines 209–210)

Reading Skill

1. a; **2.** d; **3.** d; **4.** b (paragraphs P and Q); **5.** c

Vocabulary Practice

A. 1. securing; **2.** territory; **3.** coded; **4.** coherent; **5.** aggregate; **6.** criteria; **7.** protocols
B. 1. imitate; **2.** coherent; **3.** criteria; **4.** index; **5.** secure; **6.** aggregate; **7.** faculty; **8.** territory

Teaching Notes

Before You Read

Have students look at the photo and the captions before they do the exercises. Ask: *Have you ever seen a swarm of bees? How did it make you feel? What other animals seem to swarm? Do people ever do anything like a swarm? When or where?*

A. Quiz and Discussion: To help students expand their vocabulary, put them in pairs or small groups to list other names for groups of animals, consulting dictionaries as needed. Some common group names include: a pack of wolves/dogs, a flock of sheep/birds, a colony of bats/ants/bees, a band of gorillas, a nest of wasps.

B. Skim: In the last units, students had a time limit for skimming. Set a time limit of two minutes again to reinforce the skill of skimming quickly.

Reading Comprehension

Multiple Choice: Have students read the entire passage silently and answer the comprehension questions. Check answers as a class, asking students to give evidence for their answers using line numbers from the reading passage.

Use the first question as a way to assess how well students do at ruling out incomplete or obviously wrong answers. They should notice that *d* doesn't include ants only bees, that *c* can't be correct because other insects are not mentioned, and that *a* is not correct because the two insects are not contrasted in the passage.

For question 7, option *a* is incorrect for both ants and bees. Option *c* is only true of bees—ants communicate using pheromones. Option *d* is only mentioned with regards to bees. Option *b* is the correct option—it is mentioned with regards to bees in lines 209–210, and ants in lines 34–35.

Critical Thinking

Analyzing: Analyzing asks students to break information down into component parts. If helpful, suggest they make charts with *insects* and *humans* as the row headings, and *individual* and *collective* as the column headings. This can help students clearly see and compare the information.

Discussion: Before discussion, elicit all the ways that people use the Internet. Ask: *Does the way*

you use the Internet affect how you answer these questions? People who use the Internet primarily for information may find it helps them make more informed decisions. People who use the Internet for social connection may find that others influence their decisions. This topic lends itself to further research. Possible search terms: "the Internet and decision-making" and "social media and decision-making."

Reading Skill

Inference: Students have been making inferences in previous units. The box sums up what they have been doing. Point out that when asking about inferences, we often use hedging—modals, adverbs of possibility/probability, "soft" reporting verbs such as *suggest, infer, imply, indicate.* For each question, ask students to identify any hedging words, and also to provide support for their ideas.

Challenge: Write the following question on the board for students who have completed the comprehension and reading skill activities. Additional challenge activities are available on the course website.

Which animals do you think are most like humans? Why? In what ways?

Vocabulary Practice

A. Completion: Some of the target vocabulary words have the same form in different parts of speech including *secure* (verb and adjective), and *aggregate* (verb, noun, and adjective). Although *code* and *index* are more likely to be nouns, they can also be used as verbs. *Faculty* is always a noun, but can have very different meanings—teachers at a university, and a mental or physical power or ability.

B. Definitions: Have students check their answers by referring back to the passage. Note that as a verb, *secure* can have an alternative meaning of "to make something safe."

Usage

Code, as a noun, can also mean a system of words or letters that can be used to represent other words or letters. As a verb, it can mean to convert a message into code. Codes are often used to keep some information secret. Codes are also used in computer programming.

Lesson 8B Of Ants and Humans

Lesson Overview

Target Vocabulary: anomaly, consistently, exemplify, fake, fanatically, fatal, organic, persuade, solitary, sterile

Reading Passage Summary: This passage presents an interview with Edward O. Wilson, a well-known naturalist. The interview covers Wilson's early interest in nature, the reasons why he studies ants in particular, why ants evolved they way they did, and some of the ways in which ants are similar to humans.

Answer Key

Before You Read

A. 1. b; **2.** c; 3. a

B. Answers will vary. The passage discusses the first three and last item.

Reading Comprehension

1. b (lines 32–35); **2.** d (lines 57–61); **3.** a (lines 73–75); **4.** c (lines 106–113); **5.** b; **6.** c; **7.** b (lines 154–163)

Reading Skill

1. F (lines 3–14); **2.** T (lines 26–28); **3.** NG (lines 57–66); **4.** T (lines 68–70); **5.** NG (lines 88–98); **6.** T (lines 128–132); **7.** T (lines 132–137); **8.** F (lines 169–172); **9.** NG (lines 193–196); **10.** F (lines 214–216); **11.** T (lines 218–220); **12.** T (lines 224–231)

Vocabulary Practice

A. 1. exemplify; **2.** solitary; **3.** fatal; **4.** fake; **5.** organic; **6.** persuade

B. 1. fake; **2.** anomaly; **3.** fanatically; **4.** solitary; **5.** organic; **6.** exemplify; **7.** sterile; **8.** consistent; **9.** fatal; **10.** persuade

Teaching Notes

Before You Read

A. Matching: Students match words and definitions. They can use their own knowledge, compare in pairs, or use dictionaries as needed. Check comprehension by asking students to give examples of each.

B. Predict: Suggest students look at the questions in the article to predict the content.

Reading Comprehension

Multiple Choice: Have students read the entire passage silently and answer the comprehension questions. Check answers as a class, asking students to give evidence for their answers using line numbers from the reading passage.

The last two questions are probably the most difficult as they address rhetorical purpose and main idea rather than specific detail. To determine rhetorical purpose, have students look at the information immediately before and after the sentences being analyzed. In this case, the information in this section of the interview focuses on ants and humans, not on other ants or other species.

In the last question, students have to put information together. Answer *a* is incorrect because he says ants are the most warlike (lines 198–199). Answer *d* is incorrect because this is not addressed in the interview. Lines 165–175 reveal that ants also have an effect, making *c* incorrect. Option *b* is therefore the correct choice.

Critical Thinking

Analyzing: As with the first passage, analysis might be aided by creating a graphic organizer. In this case, a Venn diagram or T-chart could work to compare the ideas in the two passages.

Evaluating: Review with students the principles behind the theory of evolution, focusing on how traits that help us survive and reproduce are advantageous. How could war help people or specific groups of people survive and reproduce?

Reading Skill

Scanning: Have students read the statements and underline key words or phrases that they can scan for. Then have them scan the article and complete their answers.

Challenge: Write the following question on the board for students who have completed the comprehension and reading skill activities.

What are some other animals you know about that exhibit social behavior? How do they work together?

Vocabulary Practice

A. Completion: Students complete a reading passage by choosing words from the box. Students will need to change the form of *persuading* and *exemplified.* A number of insects and animals use camouflage to hide from predators. Expand on this part of the exercise by asking students about other insects or animals that do this.

B. Definitions: In exercise B, students complete definitions. Have students check their answers in pairs before you go over answers with the class.

Word Partnership

Have students give examples of each phrase from TV programs, movies or recent news stories (e.g., *In ___, the main character's brother was killed in a fatal accident*).

VIEWING: Monarch Migration

Video Summary: Monarch butterflies migrate every year, most of them between Canada and Mexico. While beautiful, butterflies are very fragile and endangered by harsh weather and logging.

Answer Key

Before You Watch

A. Answers will vary. Possibilities include: **1.** From Canada to Mexico and back, from Idaho to California and back; **2.** Because of temperature and food availability; **3.** Geese, salmon, wildebeest.

B. Predictions may vary. Actual answers are: **1.** 300; **2.** 3,000; **3.** 200; **4.** 250; **5.** 80; **6.** 50

While You Watch

A. See above

B. **1.** remote; **2.** tolerate; **3.** fatal; **4.** population; **5.** illegal; **6.** habitat; **7.** consistent; **8.** implement; **9.** secure; **10.** persuade

After You Watch

1. Answers will vary. **2.** Answers will vary. Possible natural spectacles include: the aurora borealis, a solar eclipse, a sunset, a rainbow.

Teaching Notes

Before You Watch

For suggestions on building students' viewing skills, see page 16.

A. Students use the map to answer questions and prompt discussion.

B. Students make predictions which they will then check as they view. Suggest they take notes as they listen.

While You Watch

Follow these steps:

1. Students watch the video through once, and check their answers in part B of Before You Watch.
2. Before playing the video a second time, ask students to try to answer the While You Watch questions in part B.
3. After they've watched the video a second time, students check answers with a partner.
4. If necessary, play the video through a third time. Then check answers as a class.

After You Watch

Students discuss the questions in pairs. Call on students to share their ideas with the class. Note that students may be unfamiliar with the word *spectacle*. Explain that it means "a strange or interesting sight" and elicit the adjective *spectacular*. Give an example of a *natural spectacle* such as the aurora borealis to prompt their discussion.

Unit 9 Creativity

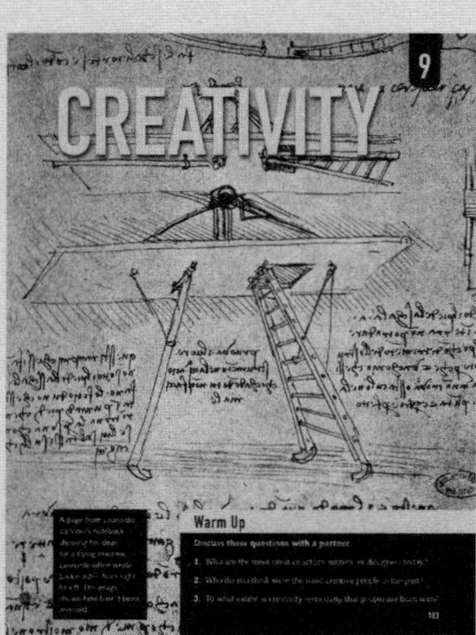

Unit Introduction

This unit addresses creativity as reflected in both art and writing. The first passage focuses on Leonardo da Vinci, describing his life and interests. In the second passage, students read about the evolution of written language and implications for its future.

Key Words for Internet Research: *Leonardo da Vinci, Mona Lisa, Michelangelo, The Last Supper, cuneiform, hieroglyphs, Aristotle, Plato, the Haida, Usama Fayyad*

For More Information:
http://ngm-beta.nationalgeographic.com/archive/leonardo-da-vinci-a-man-for-all-ages/
http://ngm-beta.nationalgeographic.com/archive/the-power-of-writing/

Warm Up

Answer Key

1. Answers will vary. **2.** Answers will vary. Possibilities include: Shakespeare, da Vinci, Michelangelo, Einstein, Picasso, Kurasawa; **3.** Answers will vary.

Teaching Notes

Before students discuss the Warm Up questions, have the class look at the photo and read the caption. Ask them:

- **Who is Leonardo da Vinci?** A famous Italian artist who lived in the 15th and 16th centuries. He painted the *Mona Lisa*.
- **What does his sketchbook show?** A design for a flying machine. Da Vinci was very interested in flight and made designs that suggest modern-day planes and helicopters.
- **What does the term *Renaissance Man* mean?** A person who can do many things well – who has skills in a variety of fields such as art, math, writing, and engineering.
- **Where does the term come from?** The Renaissance was a time of great cultural achievement in Europe, beginning in the 14th century and lasting several hundred years. It means *rebirth.* Da Vinci was literally a Renaissance man because he lived during that time, but he also embodies the figurative meaning of someone who was good at many different kinds of things.

Have students discuss the Warm Up questions in pairs or small groups. Elicit answers for questions 1 and 2 from the class and draw up a list of people the class considers to be creative on the board.

Lesson 9A Decoding Leonardo

Lesson Overview

Target Vocabulary: academy, arbitrary, commission, concurrently, deny, draft, ideologically, implicit, parameter, preliminary

Reading Passage Summary: This passage covers the life and achievements of Leonardo da Vinci. Da Vinci was born in a small town near Florence. He went to Florence and studied with another painter, quickly outstripping the mentor's skills. In his lifetime, he painted a number of famous paintings and frescoes, but not all of them survive because of the technique he used. Da Vinci kept notebooks in which he recorded his ideas and sketches. In his later years, he turned his attention to flight.

Answer Key

Before You Read

A. Answers will vary. Possibilities include: painter of the *Mona Lisa* and *The Last Supper*, Michelangelo's rival, interested in flying.
B. *Mona Lisa, Lady with an Ermine, Virgin of the Rocks, The Last Supper*

Reading Comprehension

1. b (lines 8–9); **2.** c; **3.** d (line 72); **4.** c (line 128); **5.** d (lines 178–180); **6.** a; **7.** c

Reading Skill

1. near Vinci; **2.** 1469; **3.** Milan; **4.** Florence; **5.** 1513; **6.** France/The Loire Valley, 1516

Vocabulary Practice

A. 1. concurrently; **2.** commissions; **3.** arbitrary; **4.** denied; **5.** drafts; **6.** preliminary; **7.** implicit
B. 1. preliminary; **2.** academy; **3.** parameter; **4.** deny; **5.** draft; **6.** implicit; **7.** concurrent; **8.** arbitrary; **9.** commission; **10.** ideology

Teaching Notes

Before You Read

Have students look at the picture and read the caption. Elicit what they know about this painting.

A. Discussion: Elicit ideas from students and write them on the board. After they read the passage, refer to the ideas on the board to see how many were mentioned in the passage.

B. Scan: Students know to scan for capital letters to notice names. Review other ways to notice titles (e.g., italics, underlining, quotation marks).

Reading Comprehension

Multiple Choice: Have students read the entire passage silently and answer the comprehension questions. Check answers as a class, asking students to give evidence for their answers using line numbers from the reading passage.

Students sometimes confuse the words *infer* and *imply.* Note the use of *imply* in question 3. Point out that the speaker or writer implies and the listener or reader infers. Ask how the author implies that Verrochio stopped painting because he was not as skillful as Leonardo (*he outshone . . . his teacher, in a way that Verrocchio's inhibited style could never do, Some say that Verrocchio never painted again*).

In going over the answer to question 5, discuss the meaning(s) of the title. The word *battle* has both literal and figurative meanings. First, it refers to the Battle of Anghiari, the subject of a planned mural in the same place as a mural by Michelangelo. Second, it refers to the rivalry between the two painters.

Critical Thinking

Analyzing: Again, analyzing is often well-served by a graphic organizer. Students may want to use a concept map, putting da Vinci in the center, various fields in circles closest to the center, and accomplishments in circles radiating those circles.

Discussion: Students could benefit by thinking about and taking notes on people currently succeeding in multiple fields before discussion (Bill Gates, Oprah Winfrey, Stephen Hawking).

Reading Skill

Labeling: Students will not always have maps provided. Point out that they can access maps online if they want to visualize this kind of information as they read texts. Using different colored markers can also help identify specific movements. Point out that most of the years are given in the text and so can be scanned for, but some information has to be calculated.

Vocabulary Practice

A. Completion: Two of the target vocabulary words have the same form in different parts of speech: *commission* and *draft* (verb and noun). Students can use their understanding of prefixes to help with meaning (*pre-* before, *com-/con-* with, together; *im-* into; *para-* beside). The suffix *-ology* means *study of.* Students will need to inflect some words for tense or number, but they only need to change the part of speech of *concurrent* (*concurrently*).

B. Definitions: Have students match the words to the definitions individually before checking answers as a class.

Word Partnership

Deny has several slightly different meanings. Students can use their dictionaries to see how *deny* is used in each phrase.

Lesson 9B The Power of Writing

Lesson Overview

Target Vocabulary: chapter, constraint, correspond, duration, format, incorporate, integrated, literacy, manually, superior

Reading Passage Summary: This passage covers the evolution of writing. It begins with a description the earliest examples of a written language thousands of years ago, and moves through major changes such as the use of an alphabet, other standard writing systems, the effect of the printing press, and the implications for writing of computers.

Answer Key

Before You Read

A. Answers will vary.

B. Possibilities include: different kinds of writing systems, the history/evolution of writing.

Reading Comprehension

1. b (lines 12–13); **2.** a; **3.** d (lines 33–34); **4.** c (lines 41–43); **5.** c; **6.** a (line 107); **7.** d (lines 150–158)

Reading Skill

Answers from top to bottom of table:

Sumerians began carving signs.; 3,500 years ago; Latin alphabet evolved from Greek.; 5th century B.C.; 4th century B.C.; Chinese adopted a standard writing system.; 2nd century A.D.; The space between words became standard.; Japan integrated phonetic components into their writing.; 15th century A.D.; The printing press was invented.

Vocabulary Practice

A. 1. incorporated; **2.** formatted; **3.** correspond; **4.** integrated; **5.** duration; **6.** chapter

B. 1. a; **2.** b; **3.** b; **4.** b; **5.** a

Teaching Notes

Before You Read

Have students look at the picture and read the caption. Ask: *Where is Mesopotamia? Who lived there?*

A. Discussion: This is a good topic for research. If possible, assign students the questions at the end of lesson 9A to research online.

B. Skim and Predict: Give students one minute to skim through the article and note their predictions.

Reading Comprehension

Have students read the entire passage silently and answer the comprehension questions. Check answers as a class, asking students to give evidence for their answers using line numbers from the reading passage.

If students read quickly, they might answer *d* for question 1 rather than *b*. They actually have to subtract 85 from 100 to get the correct answer. The question about pronoun reference (5) may be difficult. Students have to read the rest of the paragraph that follows *it* to find the answer. Usually a pronoun refers to a noun or idea that came before. In this case, the idea comes after. If there are different answers to question 7, call on students to explain their reasoning to the class. Peer explanations can help students understand process and strategies in making inferences.

Critical Thinking

Analyzing: Students could organize their ideas in a T-chart and then compare ideas in pairs.

Discussion: Possible advantages of a culture with writing are that history can be preserved more easily and there is greater ability to communicate over long distances. This improved ability to communicate will also improve education as ideas are spread more quickly and efficiently.

Reading Skill

Sequencing: Often a text will be organized chronologically, which allows readers to follow the sequence more easily. In the passage, the author moves around a bit in time as he discusses different aspects of writing. Timelines are especially helpful when events are presented out of chronological order. Encourage students to scan the article for information as they complete the activity.

Challenge: Write the following question on the board for students who have completed the comprehension and reading skill activities. Additional challenge activities are available on the course website.

How did writing change people's relationship with knowledge and memory? What effect do computers have on knowledge and memory?

Vocabulary Practice

A. Completion: Students complete a reading passage by choosing words from the box. Some words have a different part of speech from that in the passage. *Constrain* and *format* are verbs here, while in the passage the noun form was used. In the passage, *manually* was used as an adverb to mean "by hand."

B. Words in Context: In exercise B, students choose words to complete sentences. The target vocabulary here is used in the same way as in the passage.

Word Link

Other words include *manage, manifest,* and *emancipate*. Ask students how they think the meaning "hand" is related to each word.

VIEWING: The Birthplace of Writing

Video Summary: Ancient Mesopotamia is the birthplace of writing. About 5000 B.C., people called the Sumerians settled between the Tigris and Euphrates rivers in what is now Iraq. They built a system of canals which provided water for their crops and stability. As they prospered, they needed a way to record the trade of animals and food, so they invented cuneiform, the first written language.

Answer Key

Before You Watch

A. Guesses will vary. Actual answers are: **1.** sun; **2.** mountain; **3.** fish; **4.** man
B. Answers will vary.

While You Watch

A. 1. e; **2.** h; **3.** f; **4.** b; **5.** a; **6.** d; **7.** g; **8.** c
B. 1. early, tablets; **2.** canals, cities; **3.** complex, language; **4.** king, private

After You Watch

Answers will vary.

Teaching Notes

Before You Watch

For suggestions on building students' viewing skills, see page 16.

A. Students make their best guesses about what the pictograms mean. Poll answers on the board before checking the correct answers as a class.

B. Students use their own creative ideas to apply concepts from the unit. Have students draw their pictograms on separate pieces of paper so they can show them to a partner when they have finished.

While You Watch

Follow these steps:

1. Students watch the video through once, and complete part A of While You Watch.
2. Before students watch the video a second time, have them read through the paragraphs in part B and try to fill in the blanks from memory.
3. Play the video a second time and allow students to make corrections to their answers for B.
4. If necessary, play the video through a third time. Then check answers as a class.

After You Watch

Students discuss the questions in pairs. Call on students to share their ideas with the class.

Unit 10 Elements and Toxins

Unit Introduction

This unit covers the use and discovery of chemicals. The first passage describes one man's experiment to find out about potentially toxic, everyday chemicals. The second passage discusses the discovery of elements; those that exist naturally, and those that scientists create.

Key Words for Internet Research:
PCBs, DDT, U.S. Environmental Protection Agency, PBDEs, REACH, PDEs, Mendeleyev, Glenn Seaborg, Georgy Flerov, Yuri Oganessian

For More Information:
http://ngm-beta.nationalgeographic.com/archive/the-pollution-within/
http://ngm-beta.nationalgeographic.com/archive/element-hunters/

Warm Up

Answer Key

1. Answers will vary. Possibilities include: asthma, lung disease, eczema.; **2.** Answers will vary. **3.** Answers will vary. Possibilities include: mercury, lead, DDT, DEET, PABA.

Teaching Notes

Before students discuss the Warm Up questions, have the class look at the photo and read the caption. Ask them:

- **What is uranium oxide?** A compound formed by uranium and oxygen.
- **What did it do in ceramic glazes?** It can turn the ceramic green or black when prepared in one way, and yellow or orange in another environment. It was used in a popular kind of dishes called Fiestaware.
- **Why do you think we don't put uranium oxide in paints or ceramics anymore?** Because of potential toxicity. Uranium oxide causes lung problems.
- **Why do you think its purpose changed after World War II?** Scientists knew more about nuclear power and bombs.

Have students discuss the Warm Up questions in pairs or in small groups. If students struggle to think of chemicals that are harmful to humans, write some examples on the board and ask students to discuss *how* these chemicals can be harmful.

Lesson 10A Hidden Hazards

Lesson Overview

Target Vocabulary: albeit, disturbing, evaluation, grant, interfere, miracle, phase out, ratio, statistics, technical

Reading Passage Summary: This passage covers the writer's investigation into potentially toxic substances in everyday life, framed by an analysis of his own blood conducted by a Swedish researcher. The writer discusses a number of known toxins, including those that have been banned (DDT), and those that are still being investigated. He also compares some of the regulations in Europe and in the U.S.

Answer Key

Before You Read

A. 1. compound; **2.** pollutants; **3.** Exposure
B. He's having a chemical analysis of his blood done to see his level of PBDEs.

Reading Comprehension

1. b; **2.** d (lines 57–61); **3.** a (lines 93–99); **4.** b; **5.** d; **6.** b; **7.** d (paragraph P)

Reading Skill

1. F; **2.** F; **3.** T; **4.** F; **5.** T; **6.** F; **7.** F; **8.** T

Vocabulary Practice

A. 1. albeit; **2.** disturbing; **3.** evaluate; **4.** statistics; **5.** phase out; **6.** interfere; **7.** ratio
B. 1. miracle; **2.** disturbing; **3.** technical; **4.** albeit; **5.** phase out; **6.** interfere; **7.** ratio; **8.** grant; **9.** statistics; **10.** evaluate

Teaching Notes

Before You Read

Have students look at the picture and read the caption. Ask: *What are pesticides? How do they make their way up the food chain? What can you do if you don't want to eat food contaminated by pesticides? Do you try to eat organic food? Why or why not?*

A. Matching: Students scan the reading for the words in the box to guess their meanings.

B. Read and Predict: Remind students that the first couple of paragraphs of a passage often include the thesis and/or lay out the main focus of the text.

Reading Comprehension

Multiple Choice: Have students read the entire passage silently and answer the comprehension questions. Check answers as a class, asking students to give evidence for their answers using line numbers or paragraphs from the reading passage.

In the question about purpose (1), students can rule out *d* because the writer presents a case that sometimes the good outweighs the bad. Of the remaining three options, *b* is the best answer. Have students focus on the introduction and conclusion as these are the places writers typically sum up their main points and indicate their purpose.

Students have to understand the use of statistics to correctly answer 3—recognizing that *ten-fold* means ten times as much whereas *62%* is not even twice as much. The cohesion question (6) may also pose problems for students. Ask students to identify the clues in the sentence that show connections between ideas (*after all* meaning *nevertheless,* suggesting contrast; *either* indicating a comparison: *prospect* somewhat similar in meaning to *option*). These clues suggest that *b* is the best answer.

Critical Thinking

Evaluating: Students can use a T-chart to contrast the arguments for and against. For greater challenge, have students debate the topic, with half arguing for the statement and half against.

Discussion: First, to generate as many ideas as possible for discussion, have students brainstorm all of the areas of their lives in which they might come into contact with chemicals (e.g., *personal care products, food and drink, clothing, household products, work environment, outdoor environment*).

Reading Skill

Scanning/Classification: Words and phrases that indicate doubt or uncertainty are sometimes called hedges. They include modals (e.g., *might, may, could*), adverbs (e.g., *possibly, maybe, probably, theoretically*), quantifiers (e.g., *some, many, most of*), and reporting verbs (e.g., *believe, think, suggest, indicate, argue for*).

For the statements that refer to theories, students should notice these hedges:

3. *has long been curious about, has been wanting to apply for a grant, is only a hypothesis*

5. *are rising mysteriously, some experts, with little firm evidence, suspect*

8. *that may do little harm, might have additive effects, or they may do nothing, we don't know*

Challenge: Write the following question on the board for students who have completed the comprehension and reading skill activities. Additional challenge activities are available on the course website.

Why do you think Europe has stricter regulations regarding possible toxins than the U.S.? Which approach do you agree with?

Vocabulary Practice

A. Completion: Have students look at the picture and read the caption to predict the content of the passage. The words are in the same form as in the passage. *Phase out* is a separable phrasal verb. In the exercise, the two parts remain together, but they are separated in the passage by the object. *Albeit* is presented in the Usage box. If students have difficulty with it, refer them to the box here.

B. Definitions: Students do not need to change the form of the words in the box. For additional challenge, have students work in pairs to add other word forms (e.g., *miraculous, disturbance, technicality, interference*). Then have students ask and answer questions about the information in part A using other word forms in their answers where possible.

Usage

Albeit is often used directly before an adjectival or adverbial phrase. For example: *They had a wonderful, albeit expensive, vacation*. Or, *He was happy to buy the ring, albeit at a higher price than he had expected.*

Lesson 10B Element Hunters

Lesson Overview

Target Vocabulary: application, attribute, bind, charge, collision, counterpart, dispute, prevail, quest, trustworthy

Reading Passage Summary: This passage covers the search for existing and new elements. It begins with a description of the work of Mendeleyev who created the periodic table, recognizing that the weights of the elements said something about their organization. The first 92 elements, all existing naturally on Earth, were discovered by 1940. Since then, scientists have created 23 more in laboratories.

Answer Key

Before You Read

A. 1. Answers will vary. Possibilities include: Oxygen for breathing; mercury in thermometers; hydrogen for energy; lead, silver, bronze, gold, other metals for machines, weapons, jewelry.
2. Answers will vary. Possibilities include: for energy sources, for new technology.
B. 1. b; **2.** c; **3.** a

Reading Comprehension
1. c (lines 12–16); **2.** d (lines 44–49);
3. a (pages 220–221); **4.** a (lines 91–94);
5. c (lines 100–103); **6.** c; **7.** b

Reading Skill
1. a. Glenn Seaborg; **b.** the plutonium bomb;
c. at the end of the war
2. a. Berkeley and Dubna; **b.** element 106;
c. by shooting light atoms against heavy ones;
d. they joined to create a single superheavy nucleus

Vocabulary Practice
A. 1. quest; **2.** collide; **3.** trustworthy;
4. charged; **5.** attributes
B. 1. b; **2.** b; **3.** a; **4.** a; **5.** a; **6.** a

Teaching Notes

Before You Read

Have students look at the picture and read the caption. Have them look at the picture on page 217 to help them answer the first question in part A.

A. Discussion: Make sure students know what *elements* are (chemical substances with only one type of atom), and what the *periodic table* is (an organizational structure for elements based on weight/number of protons). Students can refer to pages 216–217 for examples of elements. This section of the table shows many common metals (copper, iron, silver, gold, etc.).

B. Scan: For additional challenge, have students scan the article to find out which elements the passage focuses on by scanning for numbers.

Reading Comprehension

Multiple Choice: Have students read the entire passage silently and answer the comprehension questions. Check answers as a class, asking students to give evidence for their answers using line numbers from the reading passage.

If students have difficulty with the question about cause and effect (2), review words that provide clues to a cause/effect relationship. They include connecting words (e.g., *because, due to, since*), nouns (e.g., *cause, effect, factor, result*), and verbs (e.g., *cause, lead to, contribute to, result in*). Ask students which words in paragraph E indicate cause or effect (*led him to suspect*).

For question 3, refer students to the graphic on pages 220–221, which shows the year of recognition for each element.

Students have another cohesion question (6) in this lesson. Remind them to focus on the words that indicate connections between ideas. The sentence begins with *In other words,* which indicates that what follows will be a paraphrase of the sentence before.

Finding the correct answer to question 7 again requires students to understand the graphic on pages 220–221. If students have difficulty, have the class as a whole turn to the graphic. Then ask questions to check comprehension: *How many elements were discovered in the 1980s?* [1] *How many in the 1990s?* [3] *Were they discovered before or after 1995?* [before]

Critical Thinking

Analyzing: Students should recognize that World War II provided an impetus for scientists to create advanced weaponry which capitalized on the discovery of plutonium. The Cold War rivalry between the U.S. and Russia led to the discovery of even more elements.

Discussion: This discussion could benefit from further research outside the classroom. Have students identify areas of research in which scientists compete to make discoveries. They might include disease control, technology, and space exploration, among others. Students choose one topic and research the degree to which scientists compete or collaborate and find specific examples to share with the class.

Reading Skill

Analyzing: Suggest students mark separate clauses when possible by hunting for subject-verb combinations. Other information may be added to sentences in reductions or appositives (e.g.,

His American counterpart, Glenn Seaborg). It can be helpful to identify all verbs to break down a long sentence even further. To help students see components of the sentence, copy the example on the board either using different colors for each new chunk, or writing each new chunk on a different line.

Challenge: For students who have completed the comprehension and reading skill activities, suggest they find two other long sentences in the text and create their own questions and answers as in part B. Additional challenge activities are available on the course website.

Vocabulary Practice

A. Completion: Students complete a reading passage by choosing words from the box. Some words have a different part of speech from that in the passage. *Collide* is a verb here, while in the passage the noun form, *collision*, was used. In the passage, *charge* was used as a noun. In the exercise, *charged* is a participial adjective.

B. Words in Context: In part B, students choose words to complete sentences. It uses the words in the same form as in the passage.

Word Link

Counter has other meanings. It can be a long flat fixture in a kitchen, bathroom, or store. It can also be something that counts or is used for counting. Other words that use *counter* as a prefix include *counter-culture* and *counterintuitive*. The prefix *contra-* means much the same thing (*contradict, contraindicated, contraceptive, contrary*).

VIEWING: Secrets of Toothpaste

Video Summary: Toothpaste has been around for thousands of years. An early formula dates back to 5th century A.D. in Egypt. Modern formulas include a fluoride to prevent cavities, as well as an abrasive to clean the teeth, a whitener, flavorings, something to make it foam, and something to hold it together.

Answer Key

Before You Watch

A. 1. h; **2.** g; **3.** a; **4.** b; **5.** d; **6.** c; **7.** e; **8.** f
B. 1. T; **2.** F; **3.** F; **4.** T

While You Watch

A. See above
B. 1. a; **2.** b; **3.** c; **4.** c; **5.** a; **6.** a

After You Watch

A. 1. Answers will vary. Possibilities include: They look like white pearls when clean.
2. Answers will vary. Possibilities include: polishing silver, plugging holes in walls.
B. 1. g; **2.** d; **3.** f; **4.** a; **5.** b; **6.** c; **7.** e

Teaching Notes

Before You Watch

For suggestions on building students' viewing skills, see page 16.

A. Students match the words to the definitions, then check in pairs.

B. Put students in pairs or small groups to make predictions based on their own knowledge.

While You Watch

Follow these steps:

1. Students watch the video through once, and complete part A of While You Watch to check their predictions.
2. Give students a few minutes to read the multiple choice questions in part B. Then play the video a second time and ask students to complete their answers.
3. After they've watched the video a second time, students check answers with a partner.
4. If necessary, play the video through a third time.

After You Watch

Students discuss the questions in pairs.

Have students work together to guess the answers before discussing as a class.

Unit 11 Islam and the West

Unit Introduction

This unit covers two aspects of the intersection of Islamic and Western/Christian culture. The first passage recounts the successful reign of Süleyman the Magnificent, from 1520 to 1566. In the second passage, students read about the influence of the Moors in Spain, and their cultural legacy.

Key Words for Internet Research:
Süleyman the Magnificent, Constantinople, Topkapi Palace, Roxelana, Rock of Gibraltar, Moors, Toledo, Ferdinand and Isabella, Córdoba

For More Information:
http://ngm-beta.nationalgeographic.com/archive/the-world-of-suleyman-the-magnificent/

Warm Up

Answer Key

1.–3. Answers will vary.

Teaching Notes

Before students discuss the Warm Up questions, have the class look at the photo and read the caption. Ask them:

- **What is important about the city of Mecca?** Mecca is the most important city in Islamic culture and is the birthplace of Muhammad, the founder of Islam. Muslims are required to make a pilgrimage (the hajj) to Mecca at least once in their lifetimes if they are able.
- **How big is the mosque?** The Al-Haram mosque is the largest in the world and covers 356,800 square meters (88.2 acres). Two million worshipers can fit in the indoor and outdoor praying spaces during the hajj.
- **What is the Ka'aba?** It is a cube-shaped structure at the center of the Grand Mosque. Pilgrims who make the hajj must move around the Ka'aba seven times.
- **What are some important holy places in other religions?** The city of Jerusalem is an important city for Christians, Jews, and Muslims. Vatican City in Rome is where the Pope, the leader of the Catholic Church, lives. Varanasi, India, is a holy city for Hindus. Lhasa, Tibet, is where the palace of the Dalai Lama, the leader of Tibetan Buddhists, is located.

Put students in pairs or small groups to discuss the Warm Up questions. Finally, elicit some answers from the class and write ideas on the board.

Lesson 11A The World of Süleyman the Magnificent

Lesson Overview

Target Vocabulary: biased, confide, console, consult, hierarchy, infer, nostalgia, reign, subordinate, successor

Reading Passage Summary: This passage covers the reign of Süleyman the Magnificent, the sultan of the Ottoman Empire during the 16th century. During his reign, the Ottoman Empire extended through much of Europe, parts of Asia, and northern Africa.

Answer Key

Before You Read

A. 1. Part or all of Saudi Arabia, Egypt, Israel, Turkey, Syria, Serbia, Croatia, Syria, Iraq, Bulgaria, Romania; **2.** The sultan of the Ottoman Empire; he lived from 1494–1566; **3.** Constantinople, Istanbul, access to multiple coastlines, along the Red Sea, the Mediterranean, and the Black Sea.
B. 1. d (line 77); **2.** f (lines 262–265); **3.** b (line 56); **4.** a (lines 208–215); **5.** e (lines 51–52); **6.** c (page 234)

Reading Comprehension

1. b; **2.** c (lines 51–53); **3.** b (lines 77–79); **4.** c; **5.** d; **6.** a; **7.** d (line 213)

Reading Skill

Section 1. g; **Section 2.** a; **Section 3.** f; **Section 4.** e; **Section 5.** c; **Section 6.** b

Vocabulary Practice

A. 1. reign; **2.** hierarchy; **3.** successor; **4.** biased; **5.** infer; **6.** consulted
B. 1. hierarchy; **2.** successor; **3.** infer; **4.** consult; **5.** nostalgia; **6.** reign; **7.** confide; **8.** console; **9.** biased; **10.** subordinate

Teaching Notes

Before You Read

Before students do part A, have them look at the map and read the information. Ask: *Where is Constantinople? What countries do you see on the map? What do the reddish areas indicate?*

A. Discussion: You may want to have students look at a modern-day map to answer the first question in part A.

B. Scan: Give students two minutes to scan the passage for names to complete the task.

Reading Comprehension

Multiple Choice: Have students read the entire passage silently and answer the comprehension questions. Check answers as a class, asking students to give evidence for their answers using line numbers or paragraphs from the reading passage.

Students can confirm that three sentences are true in question 3 in order to identify the one that is NOT true, or they can notice that Süleyman has to travel to Constantinople when his father dies.

To answer the paraphrase question (4), students need to understand figurative language. Review the difference between figurative and literal language. Elicit what a lamb and a lion probably represent. Then students need to understand which attribute is the truer one. Two of the options suggest that the "lamb" with attributes of peace and gentleness was the dominant personality, whereas *b* and *c* suggest the "lion" was predominant.

Critical Thinking

Evaluating: Students may refer to lines 94–95, 100–104, and paragraphs S, U, and W to note lines that emphasize power and wealth.

Discussion: This question asks students to compare and contrast Süleyman and world leaders today. You may want students to focus on one or two leaders in particular. If so, they may want to complete a Venn diagram to help them organize their ideas before discussion.

Reading Skill

Matching: Students identify the main focus of each section. To help them understand the concept of a mental map in greater depth, suggest students depict the concepts graphically. They can use a concept map with a central circle and radiating ideas, or present the ideas chronologically (either moving horizontally or vertically).

Challenge: Write the following question on the board for students who have completed the comprehension and reading skill activities.

Süleyman was a very powerful leader who extended the influence of the Ottoman Empire. How did he exercise power and influence? How do leaders exercise power and influence today? What has changed?

Vocabulary Practice

A. Definitions: Students complete a passage using words in the box. They will not use *nostalgia, confide,* or *console.* They will need to use the past form *consulted.*

B. Definitions: Students do not need to change the form of the words in the box. Students can use their knowledge of prefixes (*con-, sub-*) and suffixes (*-or, -ed*) to help them with definitions.

Word Link

The box includes words with the prefix *bi-* meaning "two." This is a good time to point out that *bi* is not always a prefix with that meaning. Many words start with *bio-*, which is a prefix meaning "life" and has nothing to do with "two."

Lesson 11B When the Moors Ruled Spain

Lesson Overview

Target Vocabulary: amend, appendage, empirical, initiate, integrity, invoke, liberal, persecute, splendid, violate

Reading Passage Summary: This passage covers the influence of the Moors on Spanish history and culture. The Muslims under Tariq conquered Spain in the beginning of the 8th century A.D. and remained in power for several hundred years. Their influence is still strongly felt in the cities of Toledo and Córdoba.

Answer Key

Before You Read

A. 1. creed; **2.** prophet; **3.** shrine; **4.** clergy; **5.** cathedral

B. Predictions may vary. All topics are discussed except *Moorish paintings.*

Reading Comprehension

1. d; **2.** b (lines 67–69); **3.** c (lines 77–79); **4.** a; **5.** c; **6.** a; **7.** c (lines 200–201)

Reading Skill

Toledo . . .: positive; liberal, tolerant
the rule of Ferdinand and Isabella: negative; dark, persecute, cruelty
Andalucia: positive; warm, gentle
Córdoba: positive; blossomed, greatest
the cathedral: negative; banal, disappointment, commonplace
Arabic language and poetry: positive; wealth of vocabulary, distinctive, flowing
changes to the Alhambra: negative; abused, eroded, neglect, suffered
tablaos shows: negative; threatened, commercialization, loud

Vocabulary Practice

A. 1. splendid; **2.** liberal; **3.** initiating; **4.** empirical; **5.** persecuted; **6.** violated; **7.** integrity

B. 1. appendage; **2.** liberal; **3.** splendid; **4.** amend; **5.** invoke

Teaching Notes

Before You Read

A. Matching: Students match words to definitions. *Shrine, mosque,* and *cathedral* are similar in meaning in that they all refer to holy places. *Shrine* can be used with any religion, whereas *mosque* is used for Islamic places of worship and *cathedral* for Christian/Catholic places of worship.

B. Skim and Predict: Give students one minute to skim quickly through the article and make their predictions.

Reading Comprehension

Multiple Choice: Have students read the entire passage silently and answer the comprehension questions. Check answers as a class, asking students to give evidence for their answers using line numbers from the reading passage.

Students identify tone in the first question. Have students look at the answer options and say what kind of words they are (*feelings*). Make sure they understand what each is. Ask if any are positive (*respectful*) or negative (*bitter*). They should recognize that the tone is largely positive.

In question 7, *c* is the correct answer because the Alhambra is the most visited site in Spain (lines 200–201). Answer *a* is true and can be found in the same lines, as well as in 175–179. Answer *b* is true and can be found in lines 210–212. Answer *d* is also true (lines 202–206).

Critical Thinking

Analyzing: In paragraphs O and P, the writer uses figurative language related to plants to describe the importation of Moorish culture: *sank its deepest roots, planted his capital, Córdoba blossomed.*

Discussion: This discussion could include the influence of the Spanish in Latin America, Portugal in Brazil, France in Africa, Haiti, and Canada, the Chinese in Southeast Asia, the English in the U.S., Australia, India, etc. Language is one way the indigenous cultures were shaped.

Reading Skill

Scanning and Inferring: Have students complete the task individually and then compare answers in pairs before you go over answers with the class. Point out that students used these skills in a general way to answer question 1 in Reading Comprehension. In this exercise, they identify specific words and phrases that reveal attitude or tone.

Challenge: For students who have completed the comprehension and reading skill activities, suggest they choose another passage in the book to analyze in the same way as in the Reading Skill task. Additional challenge activities are available on the course website.

Vocabulary Practice

A. Completion: Students complete a reading passage by choosing words from the box. Students will have to use the past participle of *persecute* and *violate* as the sentences use the passive voice.

B. Words in Context: In part B, students choose words to complete sentences. For added challenge, have students write sentences using the other five vocabulary words correctly.

Word Link

Elicit examples of each of the phrases in the box (e.g., *How can you violate someone's privacy? What rules do people often violate?*).

VIEWING: Heritage of Spain

Video Summary: Spain's history has been shaped by Europe and Africa, and these influences can be seen particularly in its architecture and music.

Answer Key

Before You Watch

1. c; **2.** a; **3.** d; **4.** c; **5.** b; **6.** a; **7.** c

While You Watch

A. See above

B. 1. highest; **2.** gardens; **3.** Barcelona; **4.** Eastern; **5.** 1882; **6.** Arab, Jewish, Christian and Gypsy; **7.** 14th; **8.** Red; **9.** Córdoba; **10.** cathedral

After You Watch

A. 1. Answers will vary. Possibilities include: jazz (European, African, American slaves); the tango (African, European, Brazilian slaves). **2.** Answers will vary. **3.** Answers will vary. Possibilities include: Yes, because of the Internet and globalization, people are exposed to cultures all around the world.

Teaching Notes

Before You Watch

For suggestions on building students' viewing skills, see page 16.

Quiz: Have students work in pairs or small groups to take a quiz on facts about Spain. The photos provide them with helpful context for some of the questions.

While You Watch

Follow these steps:

1. Students watch the video through once and check their answers to the quiz in Before You Watch.
2. Give students some time to look at the concept map in part B. Then play the video a second time and ask students to fill in the blanks.
3. After they've watched the video a second time, students check answers with a partner.
4. If necessary, play the video through a third time. Then check answers as a class.

After You Watch

Students discuss the questions in pairs. Call on students to share their ideas with the class.

Unit 12 Wealth and Finance

Unit Introduction

This unit covers topics related to wealth: money and gold. In the first passage, students learn about the history of money and the various types of currency (e.g., shells, gold, bills). The second passage covers our fascination with gold, particularly in India.

Key Words for Internet Research: *Austrian talers, kingdom of Lydia, early coins, early paper money, bill of exchange, gold standard, the rule of 72, virtual money, Batu Hijau, gold in India*

For More Information:
http://ngm-beta.nationalgeographic.com/archive/the-power-of-money
http://channel.nationalgeographic.com/channel/episodes/the-quest-for-gold

Warm Up

Answer Key

1. Answers will vary. **2.** Answers will vary. Possibilities include: cash—everyone takes it, easy to steal, bulky if large amounts; credit card—easy to carry, most people take it, can be stolen or hacked into; checks—easy to carry, not everyone accepts them. **3.** Answers will vary.

Teaching Notes

Before students discuss the Warm Up questions, have the class look at the photo and read the caption. Ask them:

- **Who uses gold facials?** Gold facials date back to the ancient Egyptians. Cleopatra used to have her face covered in gold. Wealthy people, including celebrities such as Cameron Diaz and Nicole Kidman, sometimes get gold facials these days.
- **What are they supposed to do?** The gold is supposed to remove fine lines and wrinkles. The metal is supposed to be anti-aging as well.
- **How much do they cost?** A one to two-hour session can cost from $400 to $800. Some facials include bee venom and can cost almost $2,000.
- **What are other unusual materials used in facials?** Chocolate has small amounts of vitamins and minerals, but also contains the antioxidant epicatechin and is a good moisturizer. Wine, oxygen, and gemstones are also used.

Have students discuss the Warm Up questions in pairs or small groups. For the third question, encourage students to think about how society might be different if there were no gold.

Lesson 12A From Clams to Credit Cards

Lesson Overview

Target Vocabulary: affairs, clarify, clause, formula, levy, obligations, paradigm, revise, specify, transaction

Reading Passage Summary: This passage covers our uses of money throughout history, including what we have used for money, how it has functioned, and how we may use it in the future.

Answer Key

Before You Read

A. 1. inflation; **2.** mint; **3.** reserve; **4.** treasury; **5.** exchange rate; **6.** interest

B. The following should be checked: clamshells, a bronze drum, a block of salt

Reading Comprehension

1. c; **2.** d; **3.** a (lines 17–18); **4.** d (lines 130–143); **5.** b; **6.** c; **7.** c (lines 231–237)

Reading Skill

1. b; **2.** d; **3.** c; **4.** b

Vocabulary Practice

A. 1. obligated; **2.** levied; **3.** formula; **4.** transaction; **5.** specified; **6.** affairs; **7.** revised; **8.** paradigm

B. 1. transaction; **2.** clarify; **3.** levies; **4.** revised; **5.** clauses; **6.** obligated

Teaching Notes

Before You Read

Before students do part A, have them look at the photo. Ask them what coins they recognize.

A. Matching: Students write the words on the lines to complete the definitions.

B. Skim and Predict: Give students a minute to skim and find the information. They can locate the important information in paragraph M. Beads are mentioned in the article, but are used as a simile to describe the clamshell pieces.

Reading Comprehension

Multiple Choice: Have students read the entire passage silently and answer the comprehension questions. Check answers as a class, asking students to give evidence for their answers using line numbers or paragraphs from the reading passage.

The first question asks about gist. Although most of these topics are touched on to some degree, *a* and *c* are the only plausible ones as they are the most general. Students should choose *c* because the passage talks about more than just coins. If students have trouble with question 5, direct them to paragraph Q.

Students are asked to recognize the correct paraphrase in question 6. Answer *d*, while plausible, is too extreme as it suggests something can "never" be stopped. The closest paraphrase is answer *c*.

Critical Thinking

Evaluating: This asks students to assess their own prior knowledge. Students may have different answers.

Discussion: This question asks students to evaluate a world without money. It may help if they create a T-chart listing pros and cons before their discussion. An advantage, or pro, of a world without money might be convenience in that people wouldn't have to carry it around. One disadvantage might be that virtual money could be easy to hack.

Reading Skill

Application: These questions require students to apply information learned from the article. They need to problem solve or expand upon what was in the text to arrive at their answers. Have students compare answers in pairs, providing explanations if there is a disagreement.

To answer question 1, students should refer to lines 122–124 to learn that the church banned lending money to get interest. This would rule out answers *a, c,* and *d,* as all involve giving more of the same currency back. In paragraph O, students can find an example of an allowable exchange that is analogous to the situation in the question.

If students have difficulty with question 2, direct them to paragraph S, which discusses the effect of abandoning the gold standard. For question 3, students can follow the example calculation in paragraph U. The last paragraph provides the answer to question 4 (*b*).

Challenge: Write the following question on the board for students who have completed the comprehension and reading skill activities. Additional challenge activities are available on the course website.

What are advantages and disadvantages of borrowing and lending money? When does it make sense?

Vocabulary Practice

A. Completion: Students complete a passage using words in the box. They will need to use past participle forms of *obligate, levy,* and *specify* as these are in the passive voice or are reduced forms. They will need to use the past tense form of *revise.* Have students identify the parts of speech for the words in the box. Then have them skim the passage to identify what part of speech is needed to complete each blank.

B. Definitions: Students complete definitions using words from part A. Students will need to use the past participle of *revise* and *obligate. Clause* will be plural. Suggest students check their answers in part A by paraphrasing the content using the definitions as an aid.

Word Partnership

Have students work in pairs to give an example of each. To tie back to the content of the unit, ask students to give examples of financial obligations they have.

Lesson 12B Gold Fever

Lesson Overview

Target Vocabulary: auspicious, convene, depleted, explicit, file, grade, hardship, merger, reprise, unrestrained

Reading Passage Summary: This passage covers our desire for gold, beginning with the experience of a woman who drives a truck at a gold mine in Indonesia. It then looks at how companies mine for gold, our historical attraction to gold, and the influence of gold in one particular country—India.

Answer Key

Before You Read

A. 1. T; **2.** F; **3.** F; **4.** T
B. 1. b; **2.** a; **3.** c; **4.** e; **5.** d

Reading Comprehension

1. b; **2.** d; **3.** c; **4.** a (lines 132–136); **5.** a; **6.** c (lines 219–220); **7.** b (sidebar, page 265)

Reading Skill

Answers may vary. Possibilities include:
Personal pronouns: *they* (line 7)
Demonstratives: *that* (line 21)
Forms of Other: *another* (line 19)
Conjunctions: *and* (line 24)
Signal words: *however* (line 27)
Synonyms: *vehicles, trucks* (lines 18 and 25)

Vocabulary Practice
A. 1. explicitly; **2.** auspicious; **3.** depleted; **4.** grade; **5.** filed; **6.** unrestrained; **7.** convene; **8.** hardships
B. 1. merger; **2.** explicit; **3.** reprising; **4.** convene

Teaching Notes

Before You Read

A. Understanding Charts: Students use an infographic to answer the questions. It is important here that students understand the terms *adjusted for inflation* and *in real terms*, which are both used to refer to figures which take into account the change in the value of money over time (*inflation*). The infographic shows the price of gold in real terms. Question 1, however, refers to figures *without* adjustment for inflation. Students must read the caption alongside the infographic in order to get the correct answer.

B. Skimming for Main Ideas: Give students one minute to skim and match each topic to the section.

Reading Comprehension

Multiple Choice: Have students read the entire passage silently and answer the comprehension questions. Check answers as a class, asking students to give evidence for their answers using line numbers from the reading passage. Ask students to explain the strategies they use in answering the questions.

In question 1, students have to determine the purpose of the paragraph. Often, the first sentence indicates the purpose. In this paragraph, the first sentence is merely a transition. The second sentence states the main idea, and so, signals the purpose. Students need to create cohesion in question 2 by inserting a sentence. Because the sentence begins with *For example,* it must follow a sentence that gives a general statement that this example will support, making *d* the best answer. In question 5, students have to do math to find the answer, dividing 18,000 by 40.

Critical Thinking

Analyzing: Have students take notes on what the personal stories add to the reader's understanding of the topic, before they answer the questions. Extend the task by asking students to give examples of how personal stories are used in daily life to convey ideas (e.g., in lectures, job interviews, to begin an essay, etc.).

Discussion: To clarify their ideas, have students work in pairs to create T-charts with the pros and cons of this project. For example, a clear pro of the project is that it would provide jobs. An argument against might be that it would negatively affect the environment. Then have them discuss in small groups or with new partners. When students finish, have volunteers add pros and cons to a T-chart on the board.

Reading Skill

Scanning and Classification: Students may be intimidated by this long list. Reassure them that they have already been applying these concepts in previous units as they have answered questions about reference and cohesion.

Challenge: For students who have completed the comprehension and reading skill activities, suggest they choose another page in the unit to analyze in the same way as in the Reading Skill task. Additional challenge activities are available on the course website.

Vocabulary Practice

A. Definitions: Students read a passage and then use context to match words to definitions. Students can use knowledge of prefixes (*ex-, de-, un-*) and suffixes (*-ly, -ious, -ed, -ship*) to recognize parts of speech and guess meaning.

B. Completion: In exercise B, students complete a paragraph by choosing the correct word. For added challenge, suggest students write a paragraph with all target vocabulary.

Word Link

Elicit the meanings of each word in the box. Have students write an example sentence for each.

VIEWING: The Art Smuggler

Video Summary: Michel Van Rijn is a former art thief who now acts as a consultant to the police, helping them expose art crimes.

Answer Key

Before You Watch

1. f; **2.** b; **3.** e; **4.** a; **5.** d; **6.** c

While You Watch

A. 1. art theft consultant; **2.** making them appear legal; **3.** Art Loss Register; **4.** saving endangered antiquities; **5.** context; **6.** Italy
B. 1. deny; **2.** expose; **3.** recovery; **4.** illusion; **5.** convene; **6.** fake; **7.** valid; **8.** transaction; **9.** context; **10.** value

After You Watch

1. Answers will vary. Possibilities include: Yes, because they provide valuable insight into how the crimes are carried out and can help prevent future crimes. **2.** Answers will vary. Possibilities include: People who knowingly buy and sell stolen art should be prosecuted. Both situations are equally criminal. **3.** Answers will vary. Possibilities include: *The Card Players* (Cezanne), *No. 5* (Pollack), *La Reve* (Picasso), and several by Van Gogh.

Teaching Notes

Before You Watch

For suggestions on building students' viewing skills, see page 16.

Have students match the phrases to the definitions, using dictionaries if necessary. Check answers as a class.

While You Watch

Follow these steps:

1. Allow students time to read sentences 1–6 in part A before playing the video. Students watch the video through once, and complete their answers. Check answers as a class.
2. Have students first read the passage in part B and guess the answers. Then watch the video a second time and have students check their original guesses.
3. After they've watched the video a second time, students check answers with a partner.
4. If necessary, play the video through a third time. Then check answers as a class.

After You Watch

Students discuss the questions in pairs. Call on students to share their ideas with the class. If time allows, have students use the Internet to research some valuable pieces of art before discussing question 3.

Glossary of Terms

affix letters added to the beginning (prefix) or end (suffix) of a word that change the word's meaning and part of speech

caption a title or description printed underneath or next to a photograph or other graphic

chunking reading text in groups of words such as phrases, not reading word by word

cloze a technique for checking comprehension of a text by omitting words from a passage and substituting gaps

collocation words that frequently occur together, for example, "blonde hair"

extensive reading reading longer texts outside the classroom, primarily for interest or pleasure, at a language level that is appropriate for the reader

gist comprehension understanding the general meaning or sense of a text

graphic organizer a visual way of showing the relationship of ideas from a text; examples used in *Reading Explorer* are timelines, Venn diagrams, and word webs

high-frequency vocabulary the most commonly occurring and useful words that students need to know for reading

inference understanding meaning that is not directly stated in a text; "reading between the lines"

intensive reading guided, detailed reading often done in class for a particular purpose, such as building vocabulary or developing reading skills

linear text prose or written text, as contrasted to graphically presented material such as photographs, videos, maps, and charts

main idea the most important idea of a paragraph or entire reading passage

mnemonic a memory aid, such as associating a word with a picture, to make something easier to learn or remember

paraphrasing expressing the same idea using different words

reference the relationship between a word—for example, a pronoun such as *it* or *him*—and the name, word, or idea that it stands for

scan to read quickly in search of specific information, such as names and dates

skim to read quickly to determine the gist of a passage or the main ideas

subvocalizing pronouncing words quietly while reading; moving lips, tongue, and throat

summary a short account of a reading or video that gives only the main ideas

timeline a graphic organizer that shows the relationship between events in chronological order

Venn diagram a type of graphic organizer with two or more overlapping circles that indicate comparison (where things are the same) and contrast (where things are different)

visual literacy understanding and interpreting information in the form of photographs, videos, maps, and graphic images such as charts and diagrams; also referred to as "graphic literacy"

word map a graphic organizer that shows how words and ideas are related to each other